FLORAL MANDALA

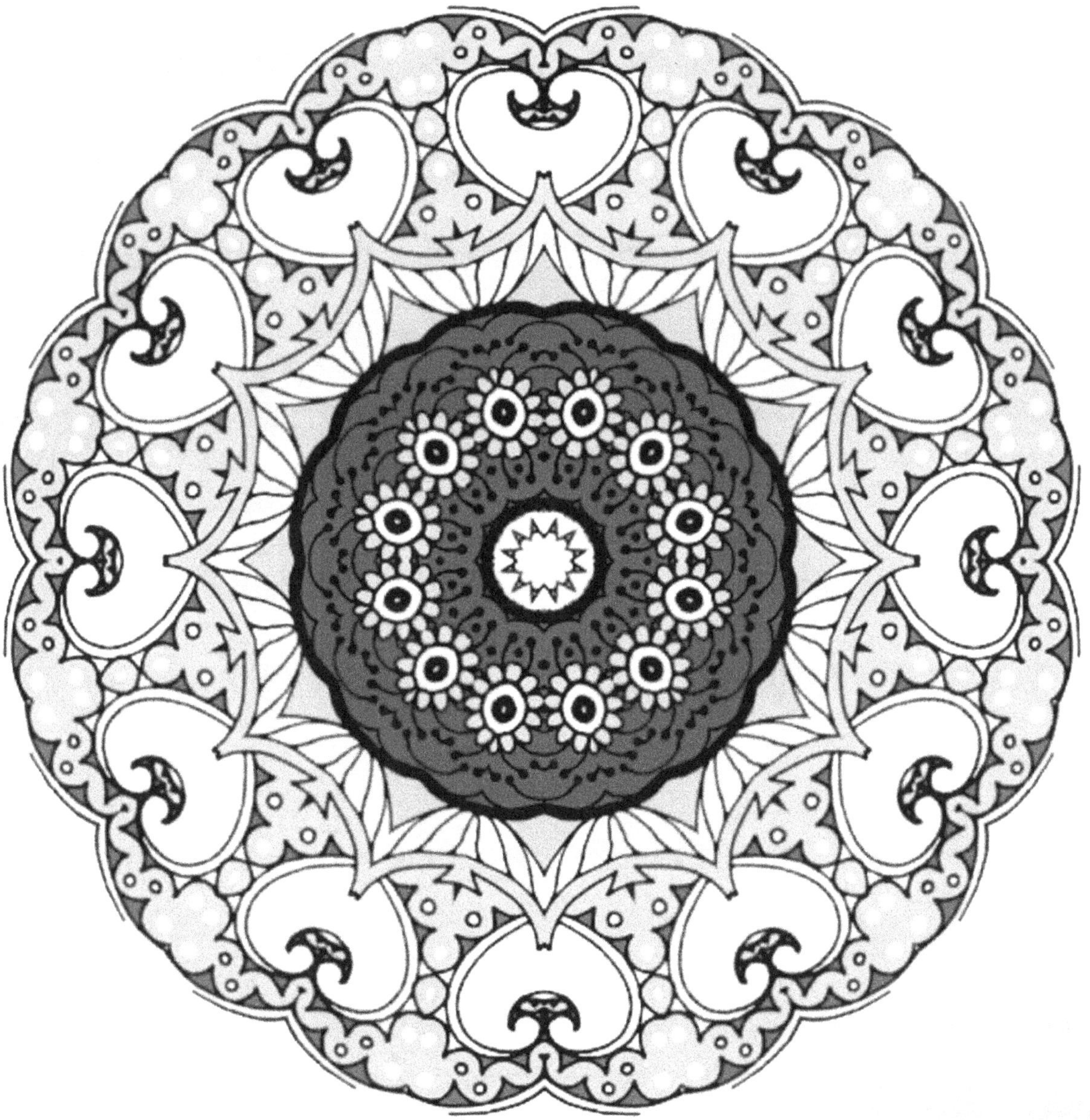

COLORING BOOKS

VOLUME 2.

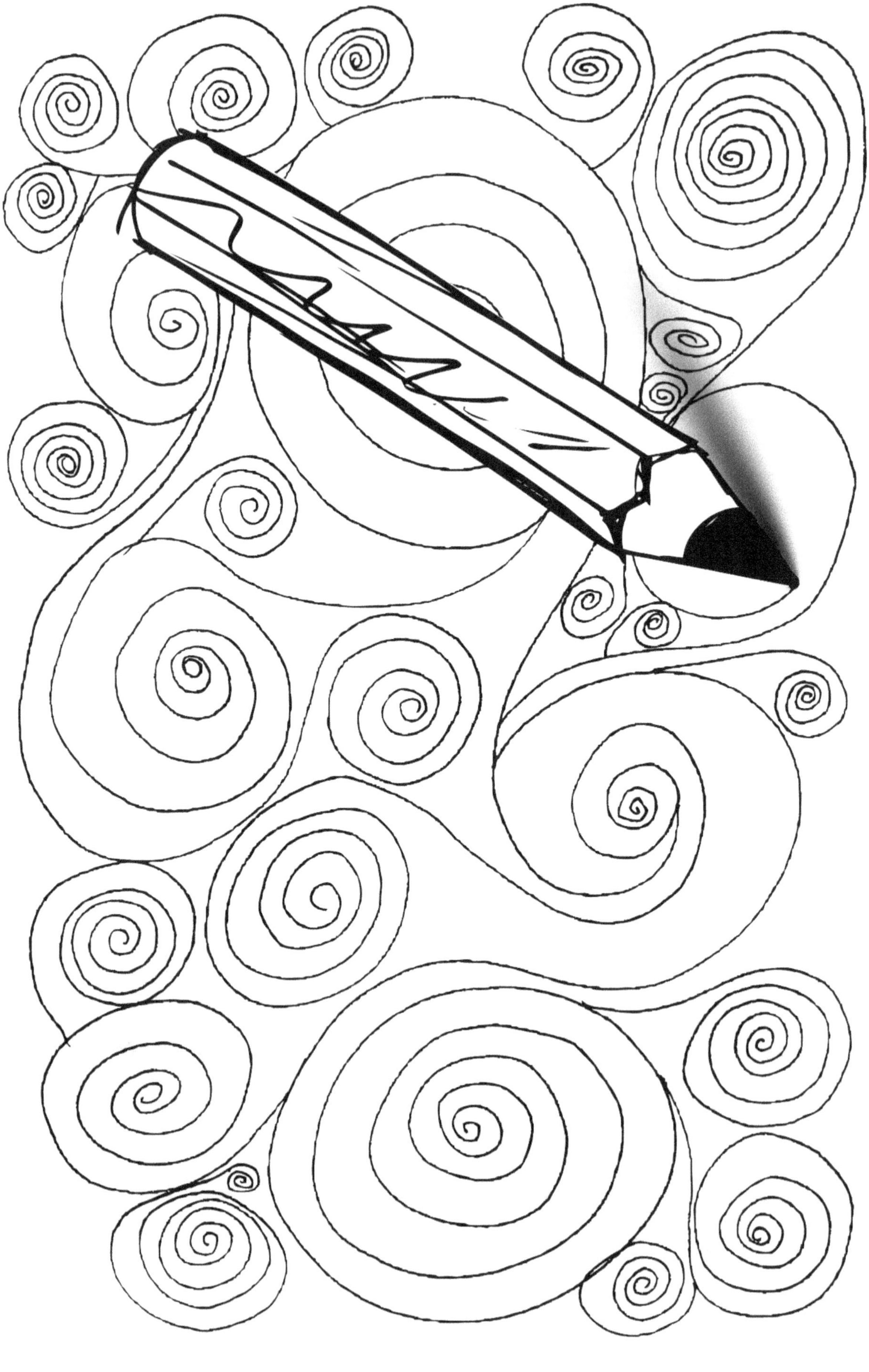

COLOR TEST PAGE

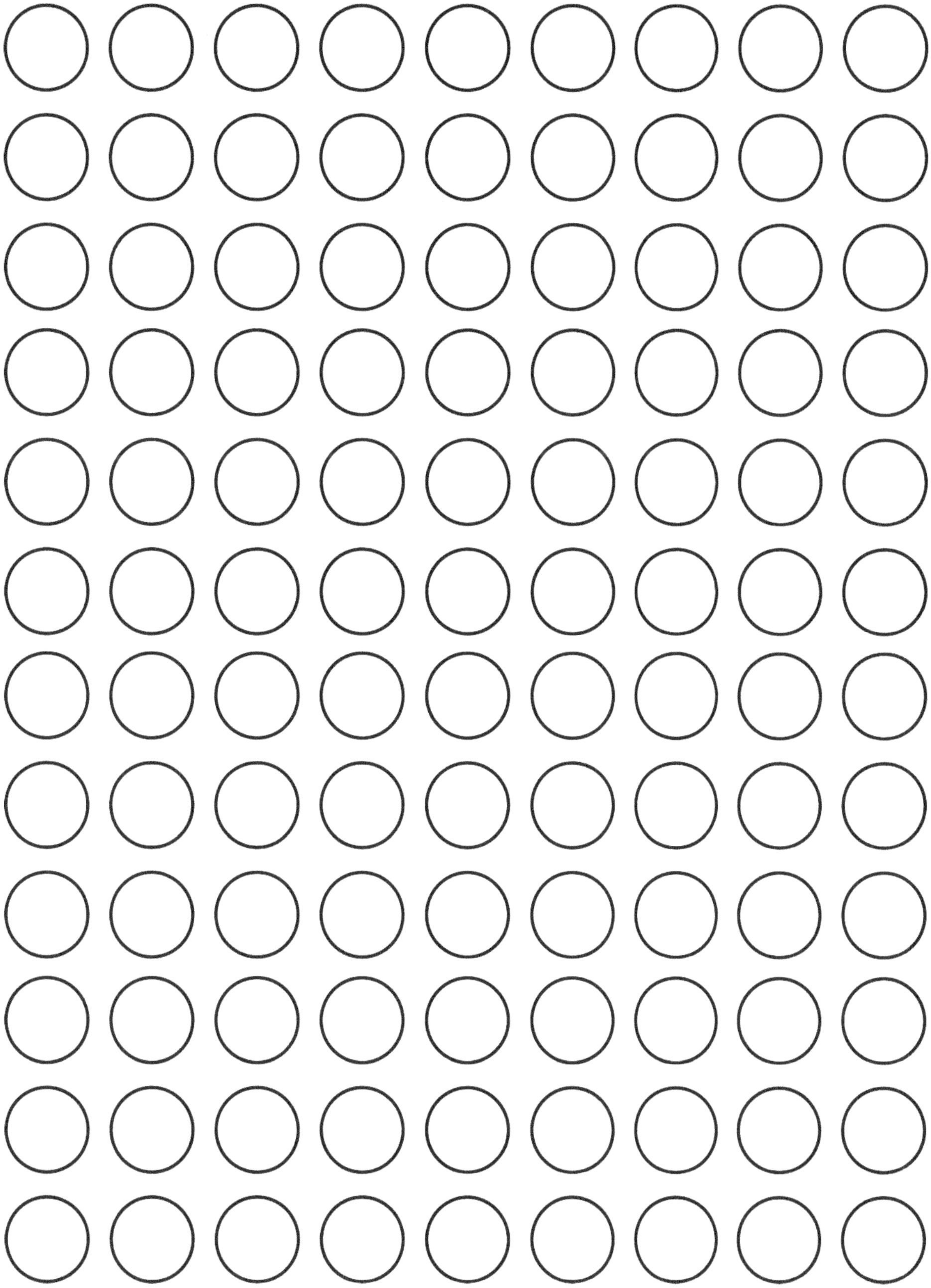

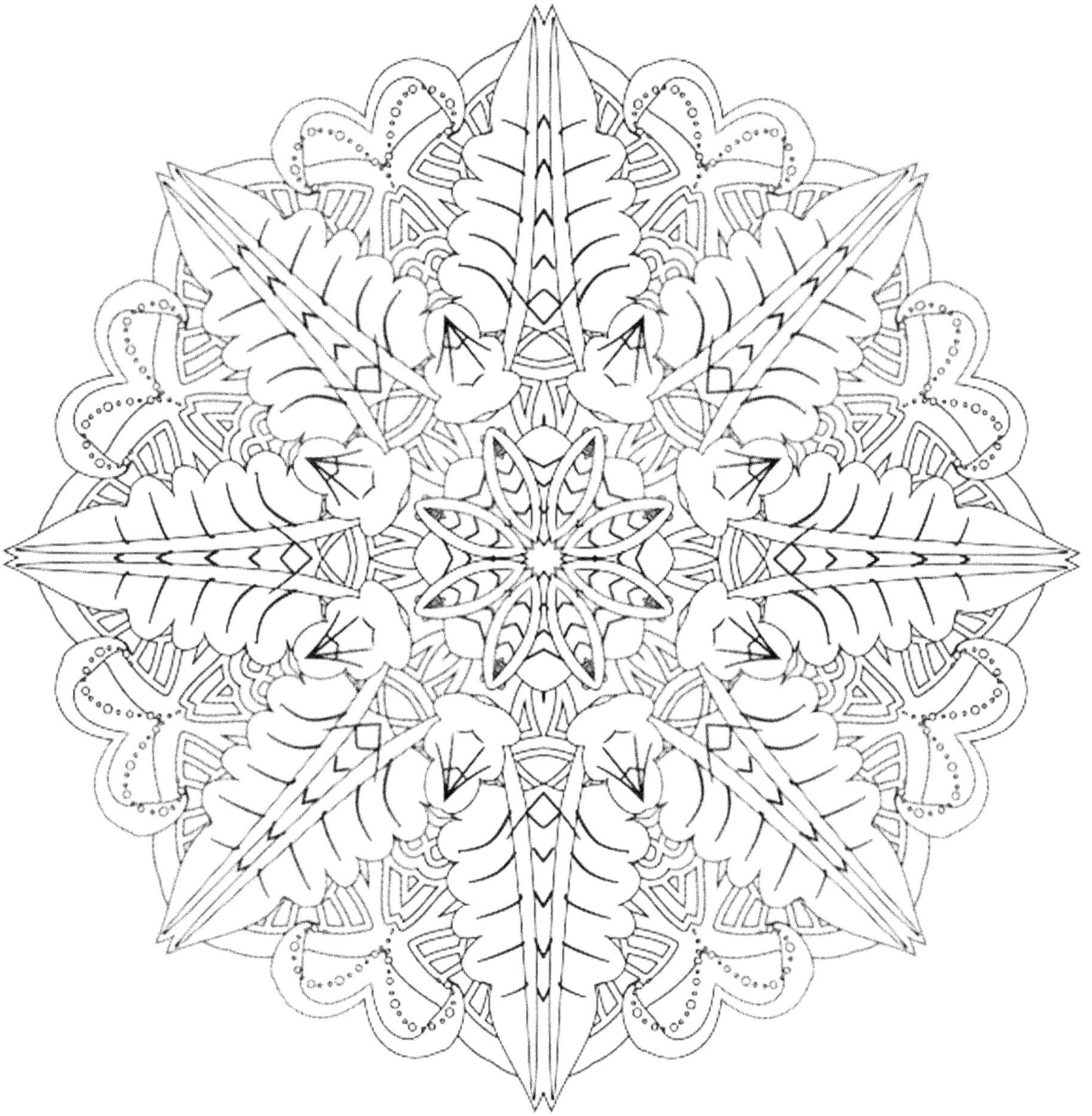

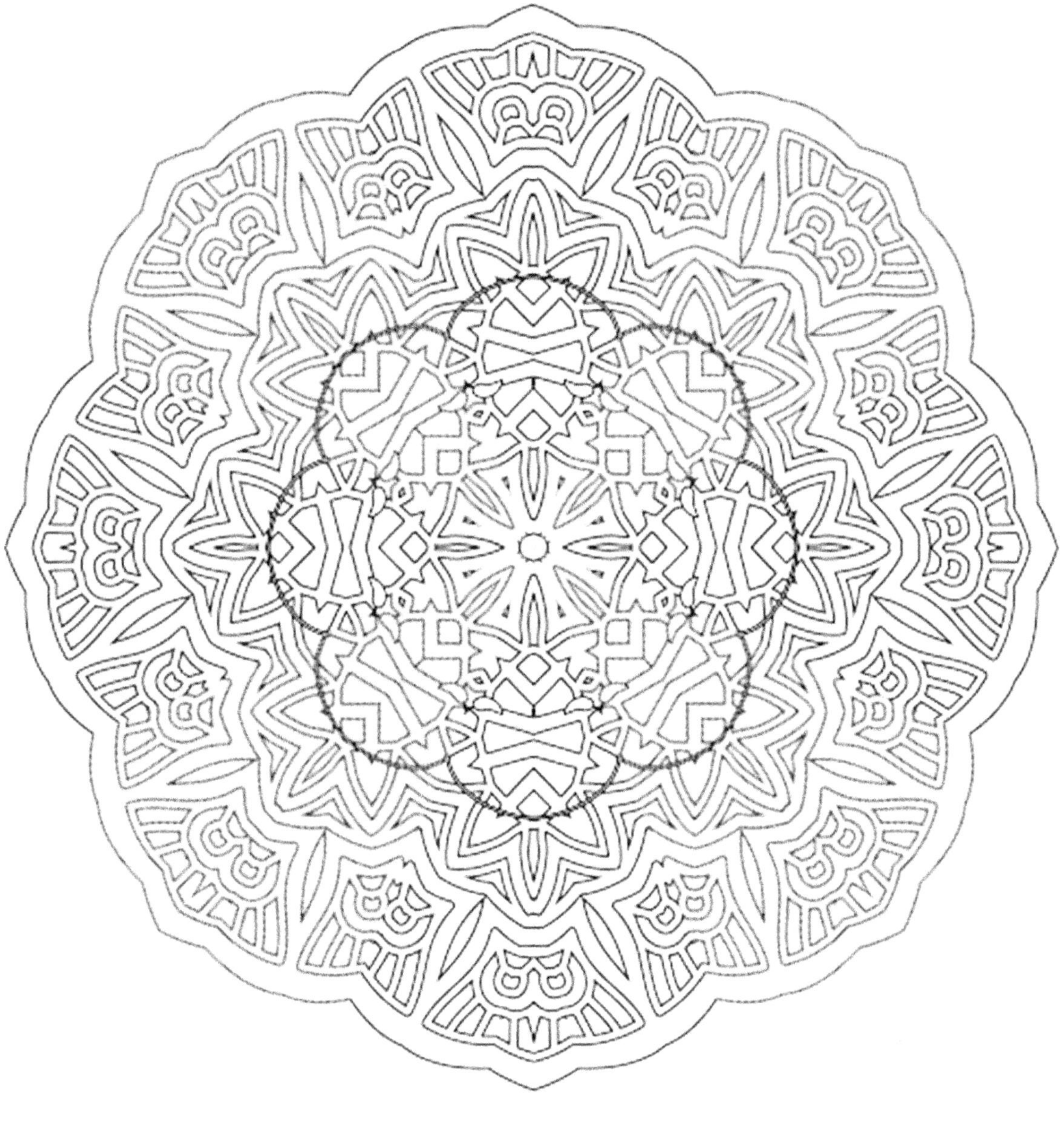

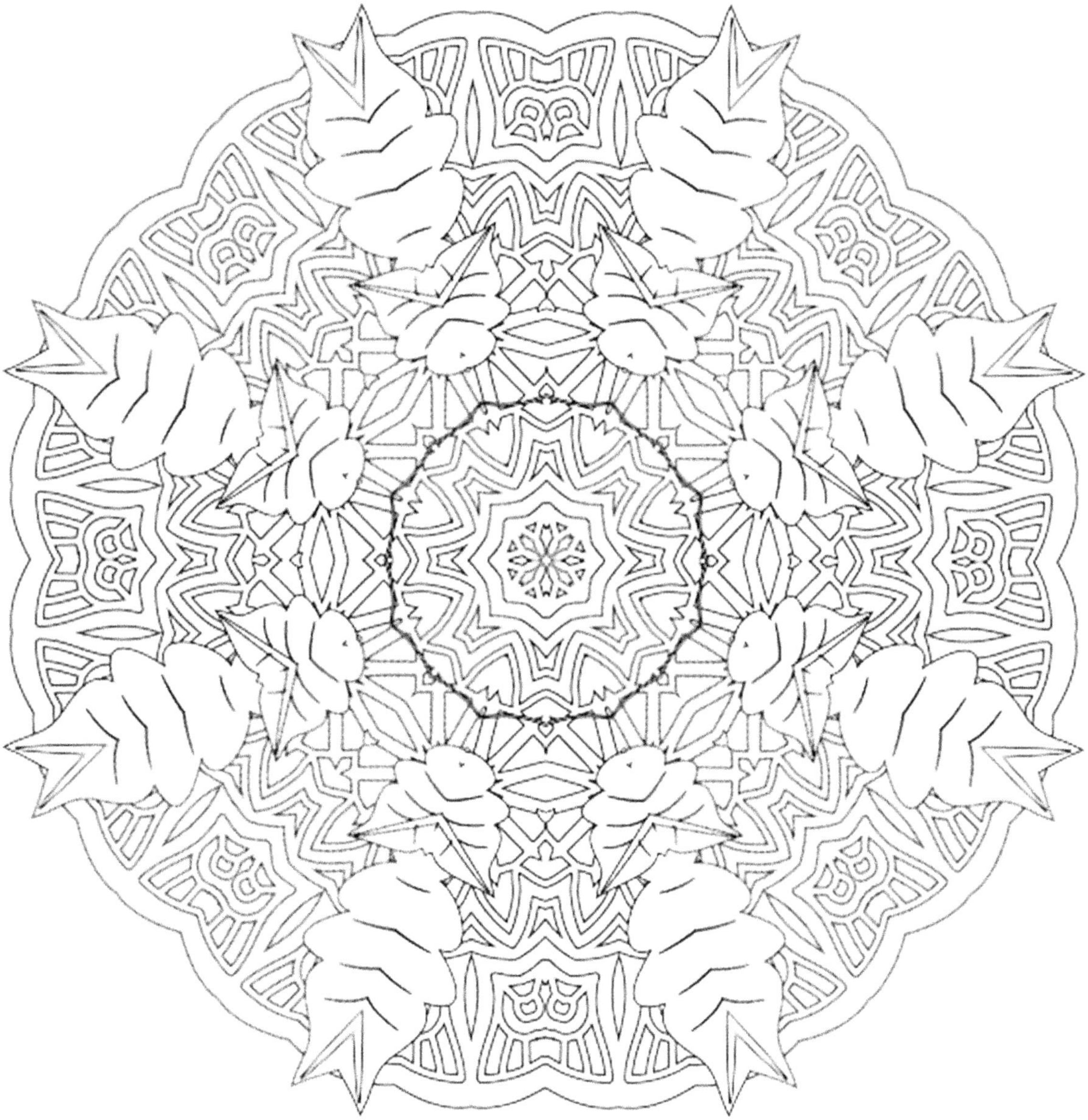

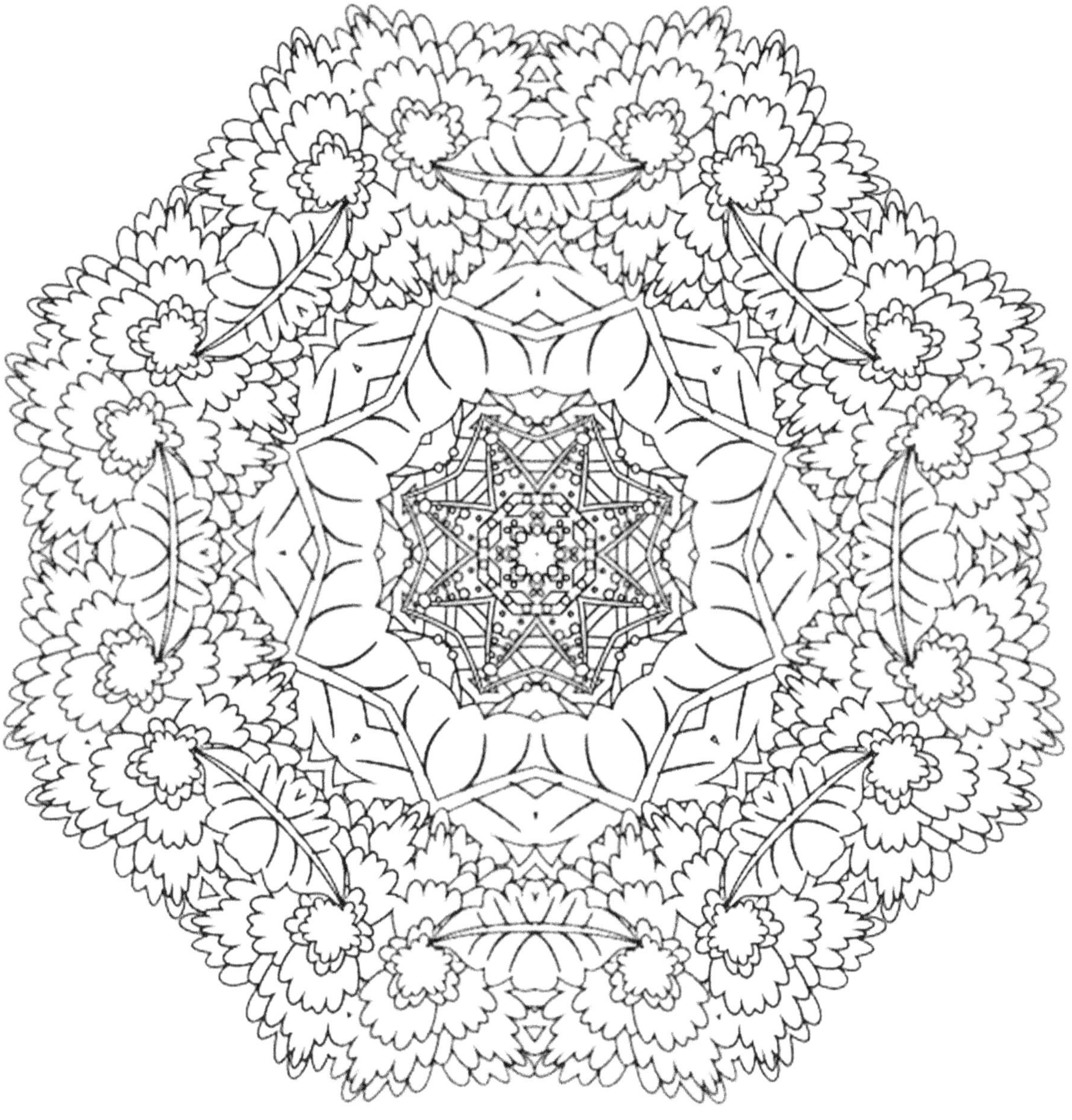

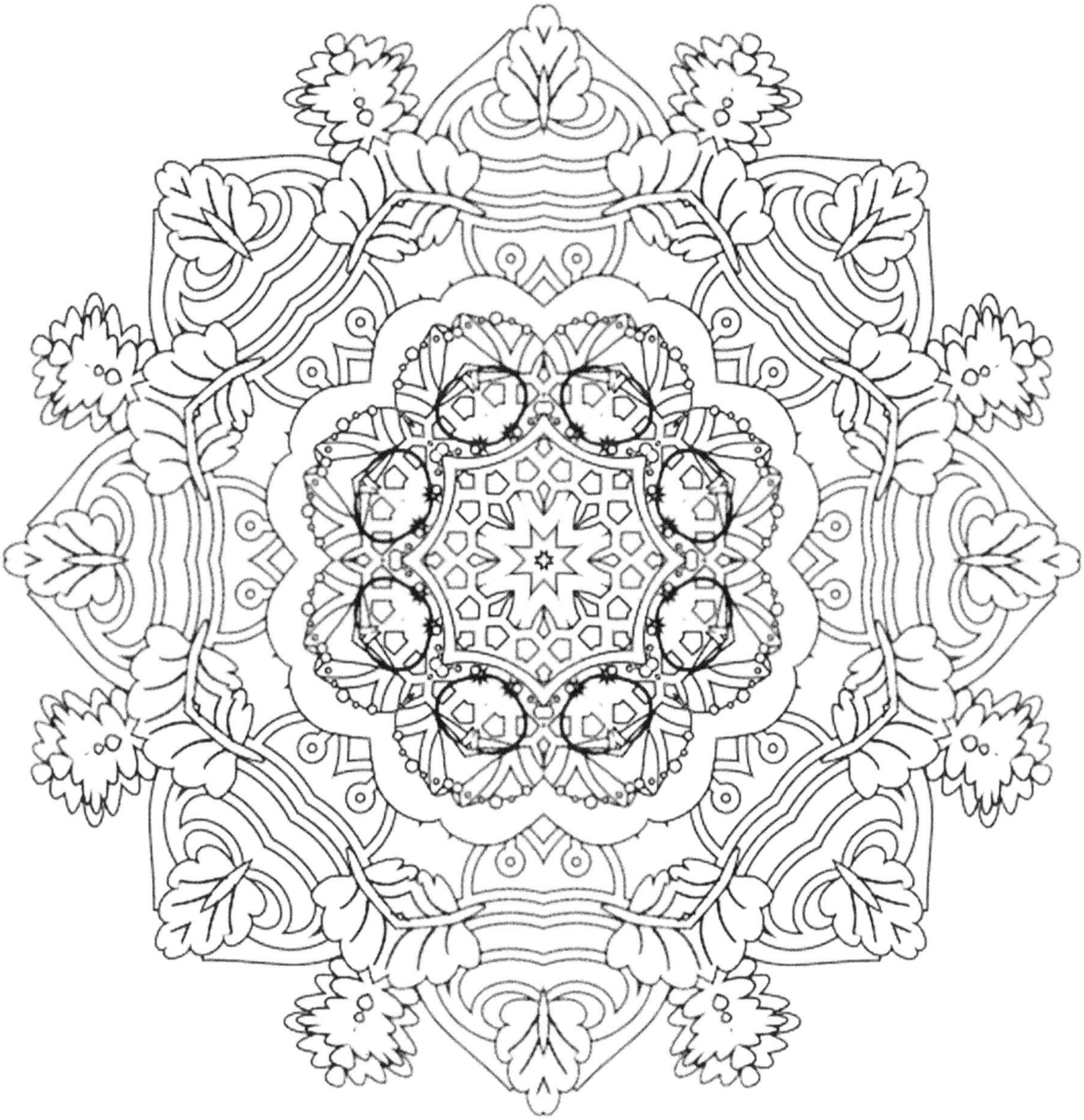

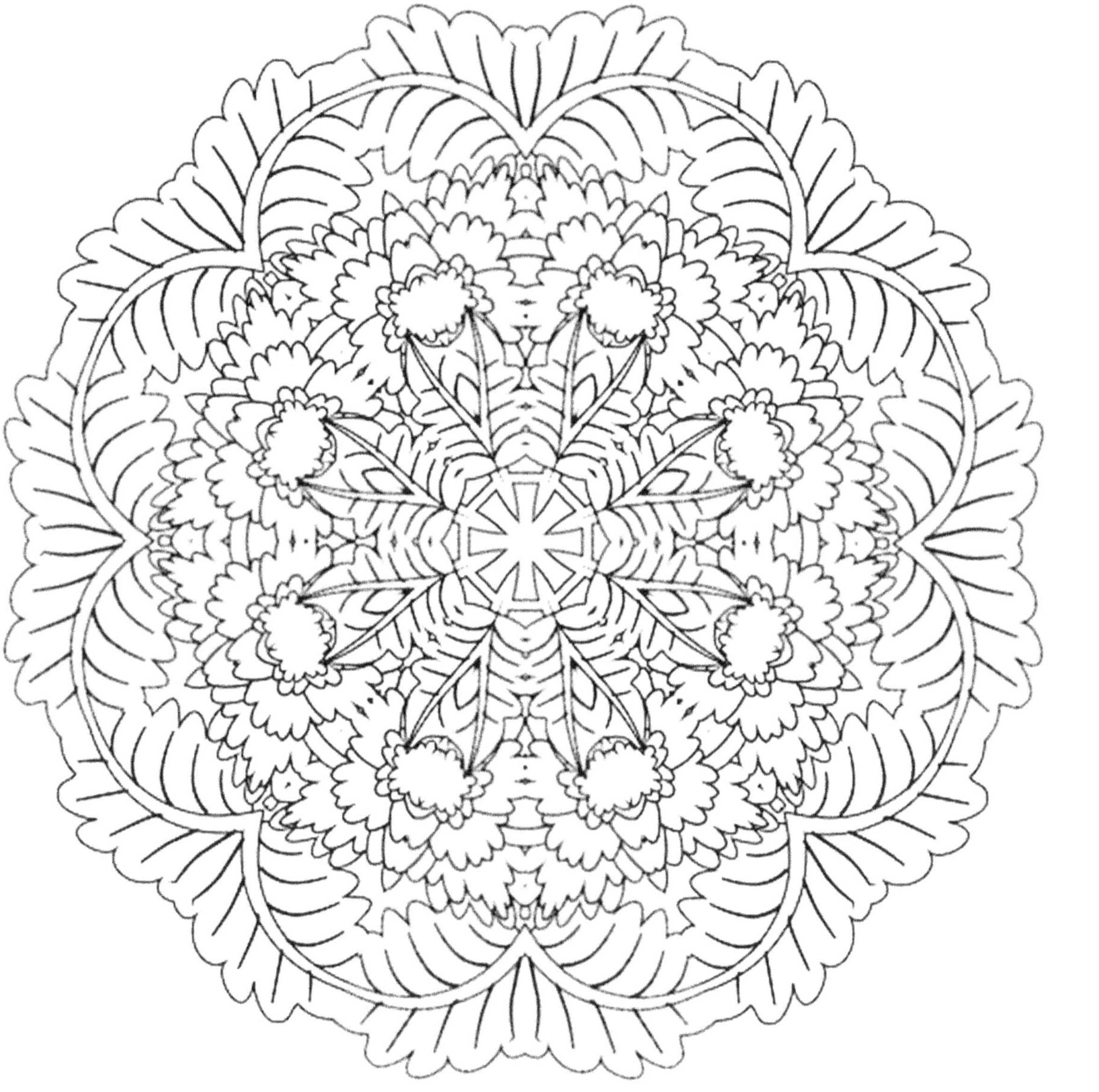

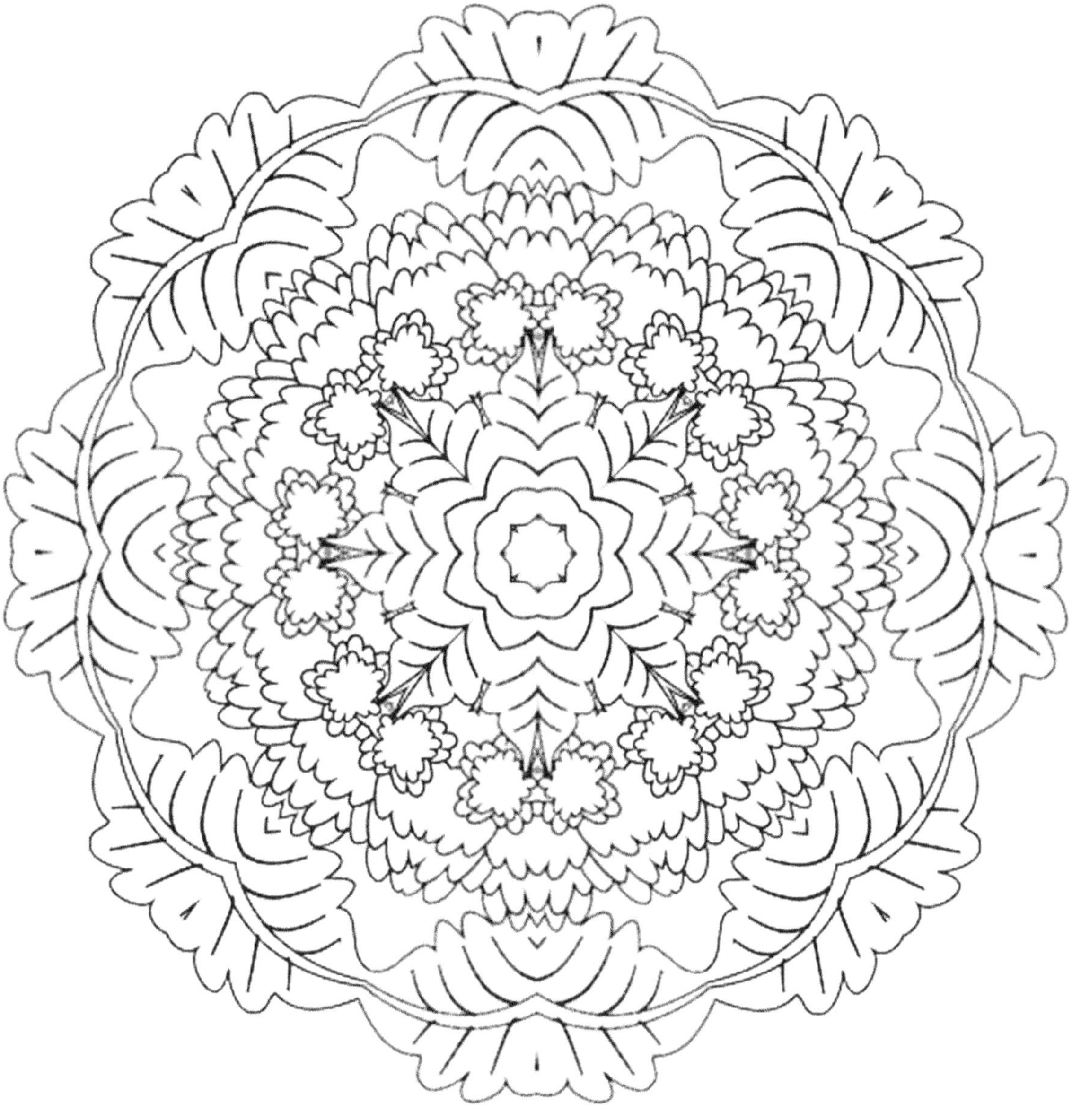

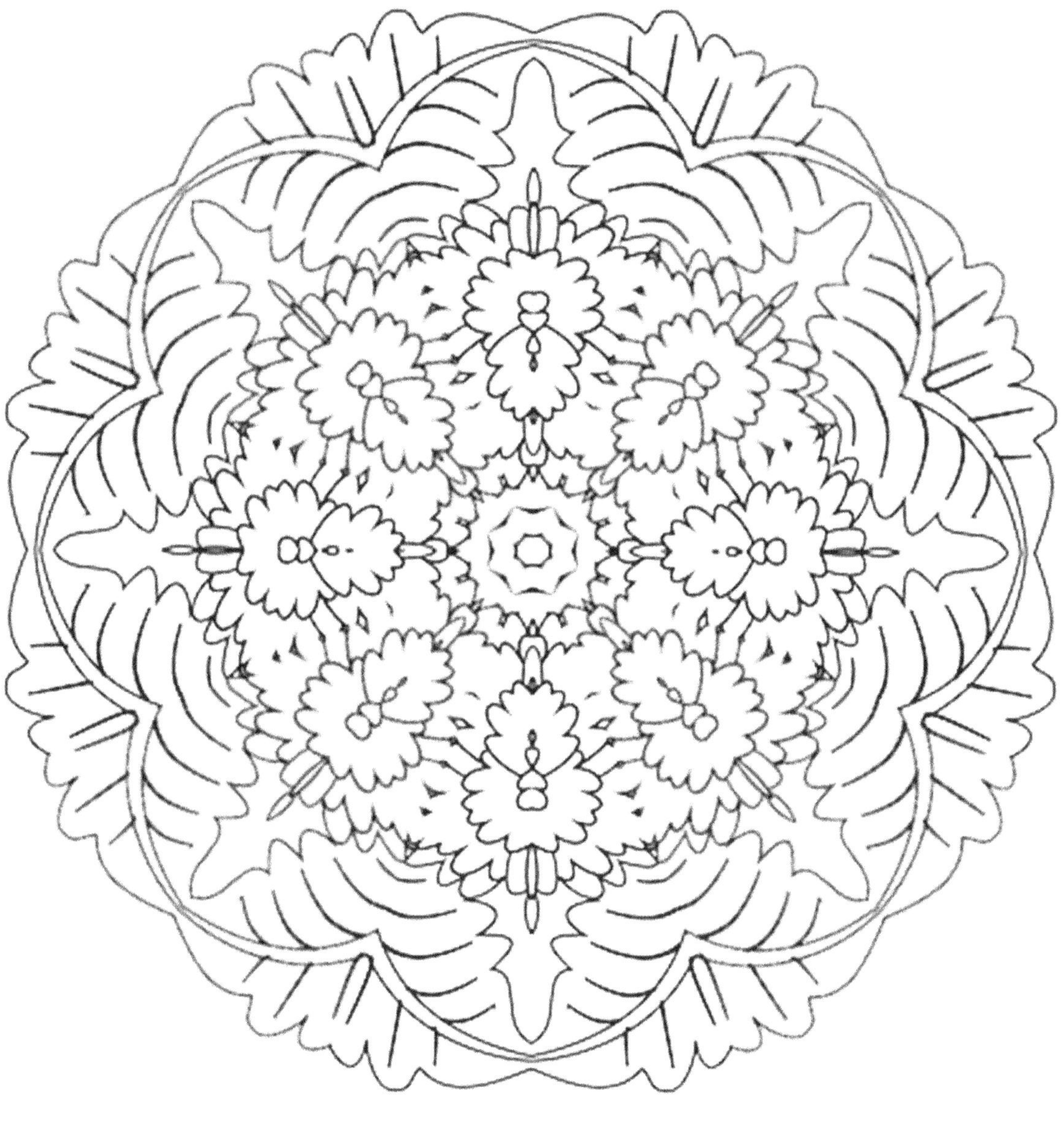

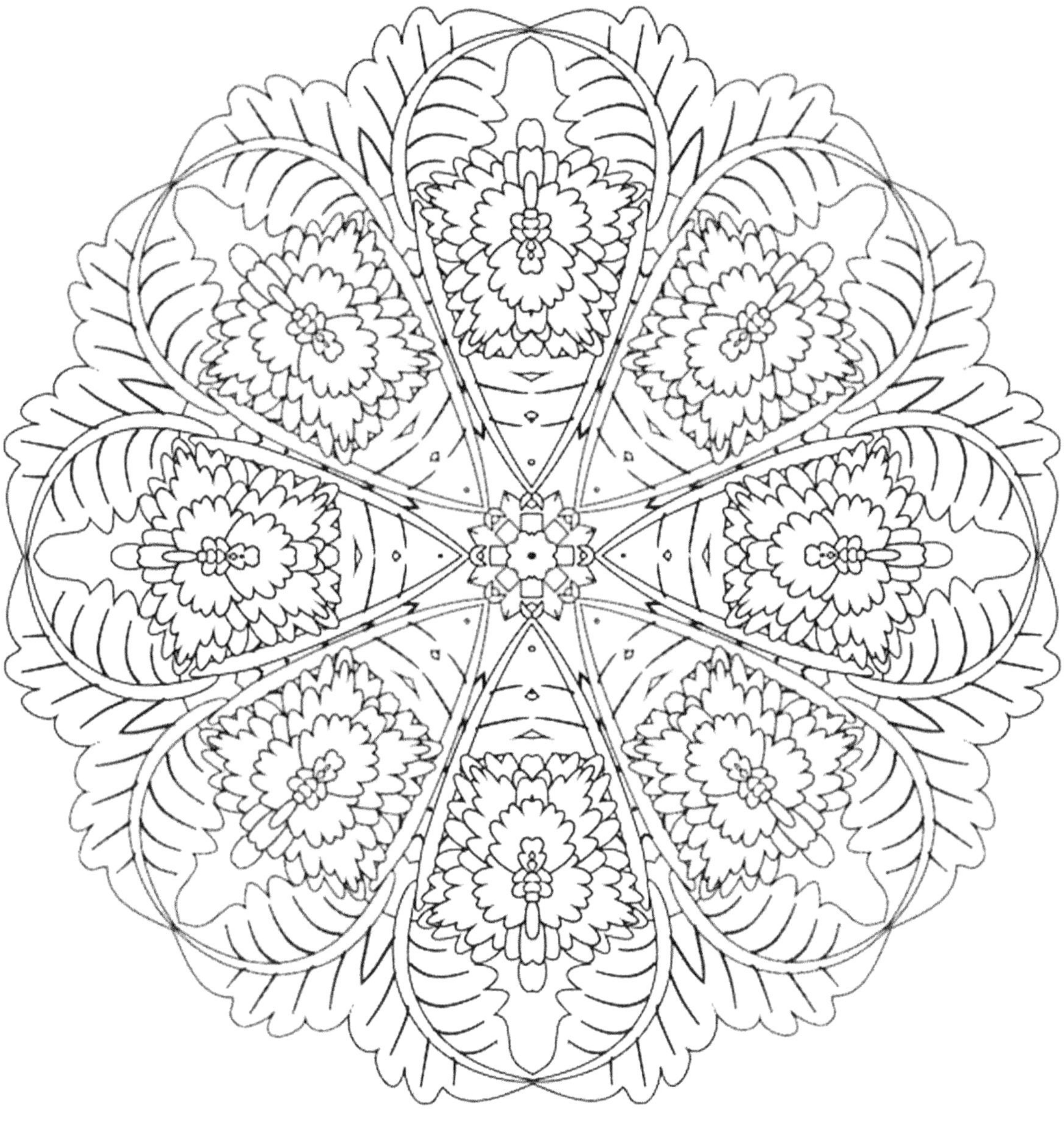

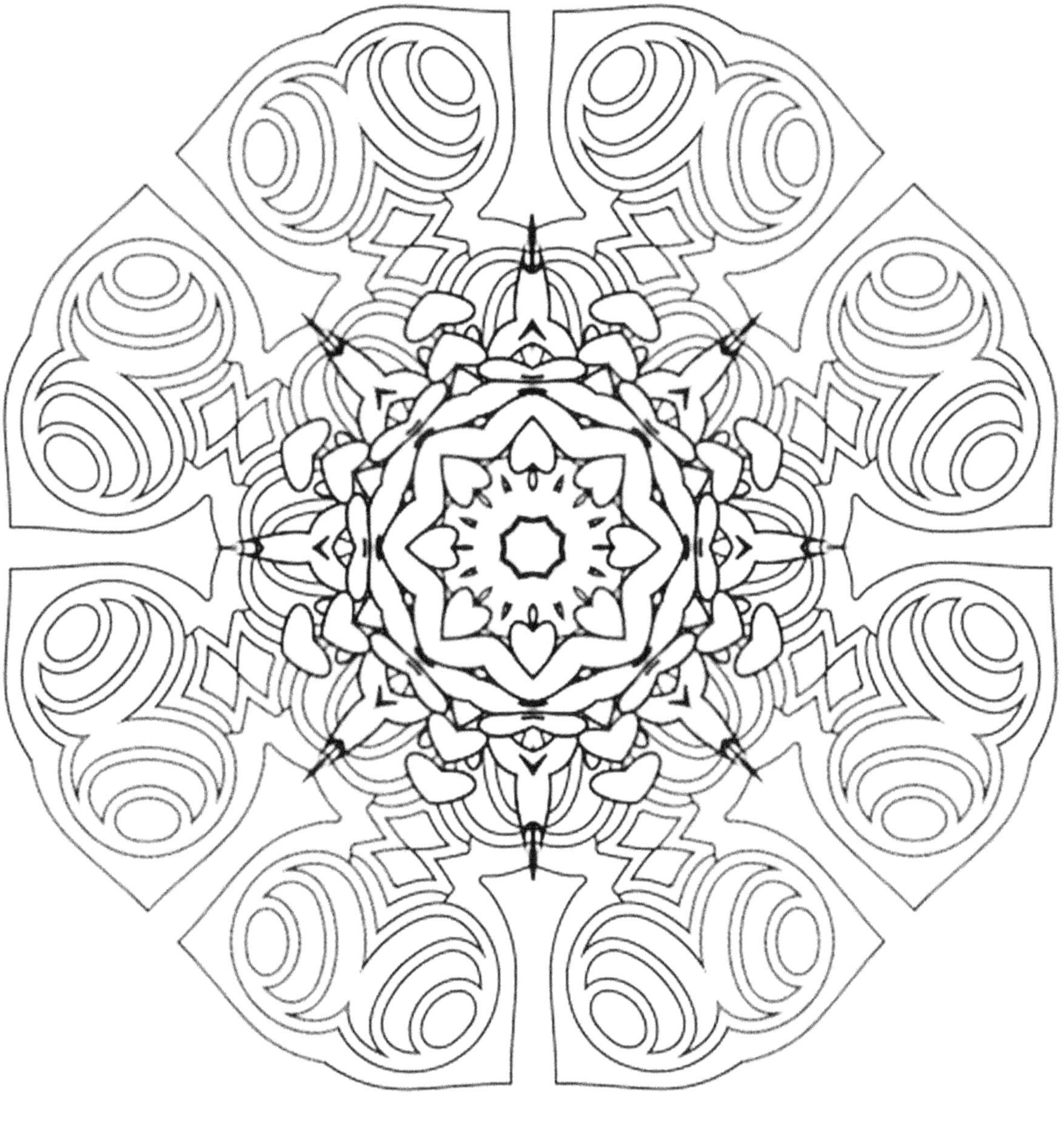

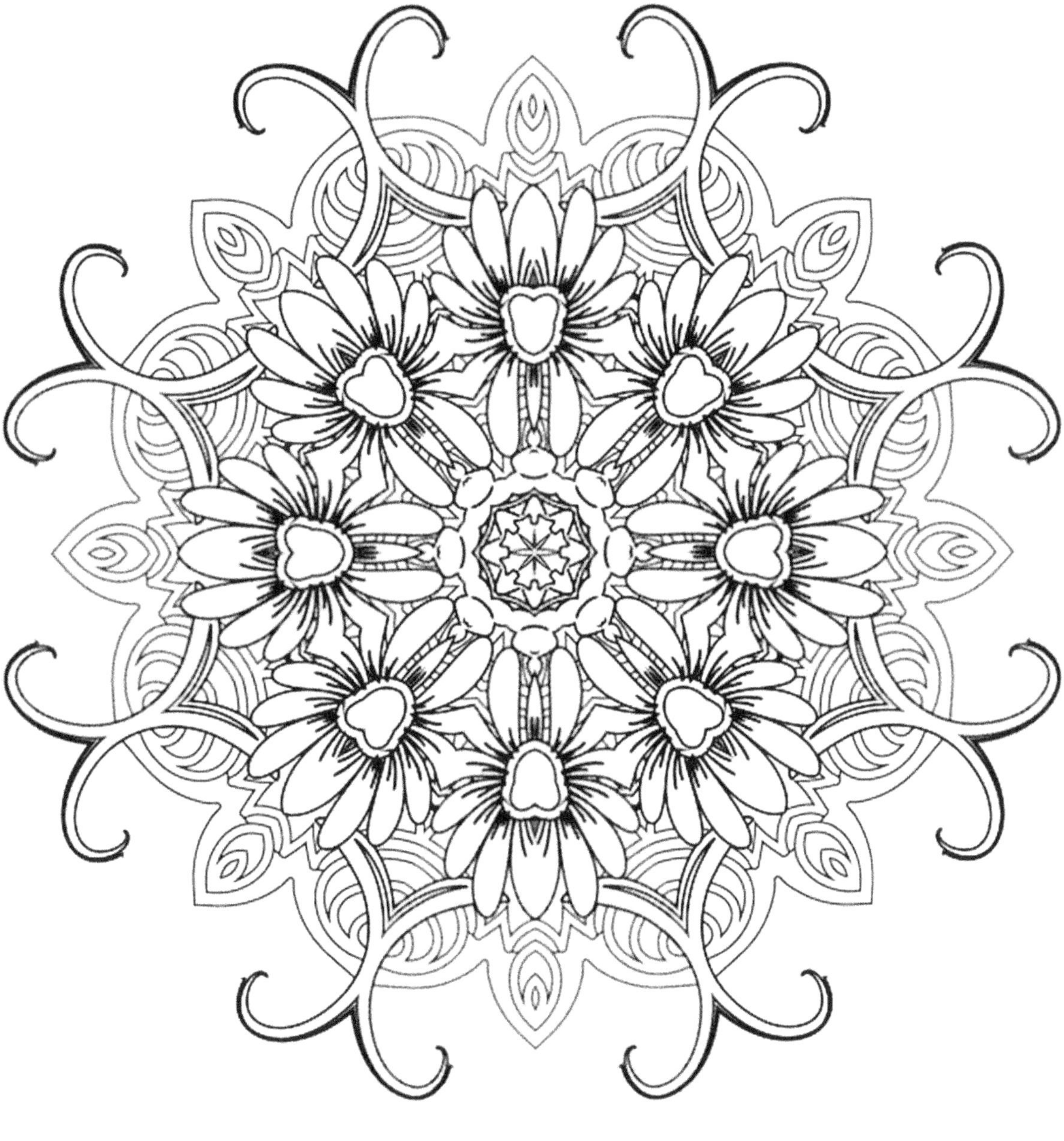

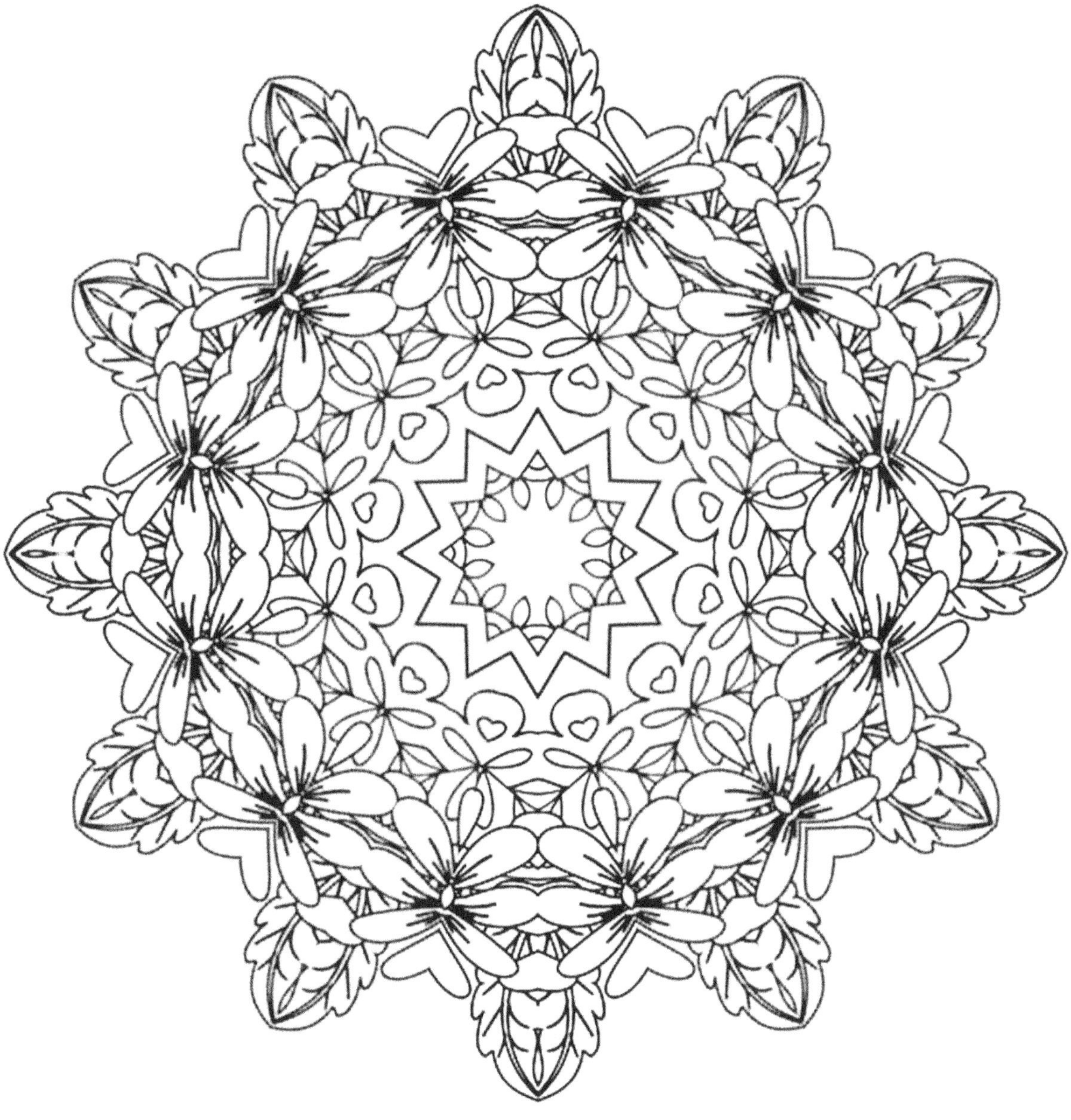

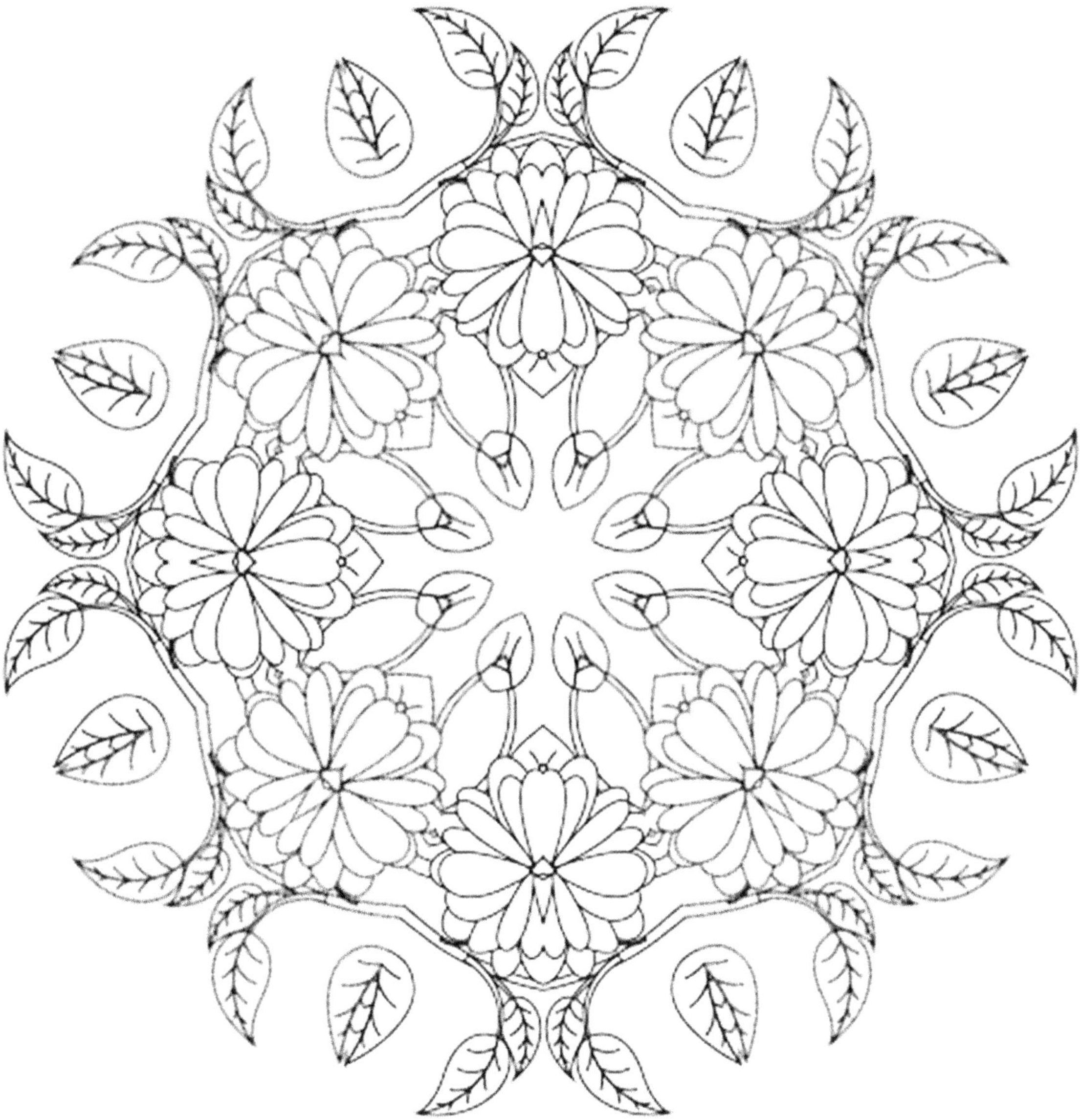

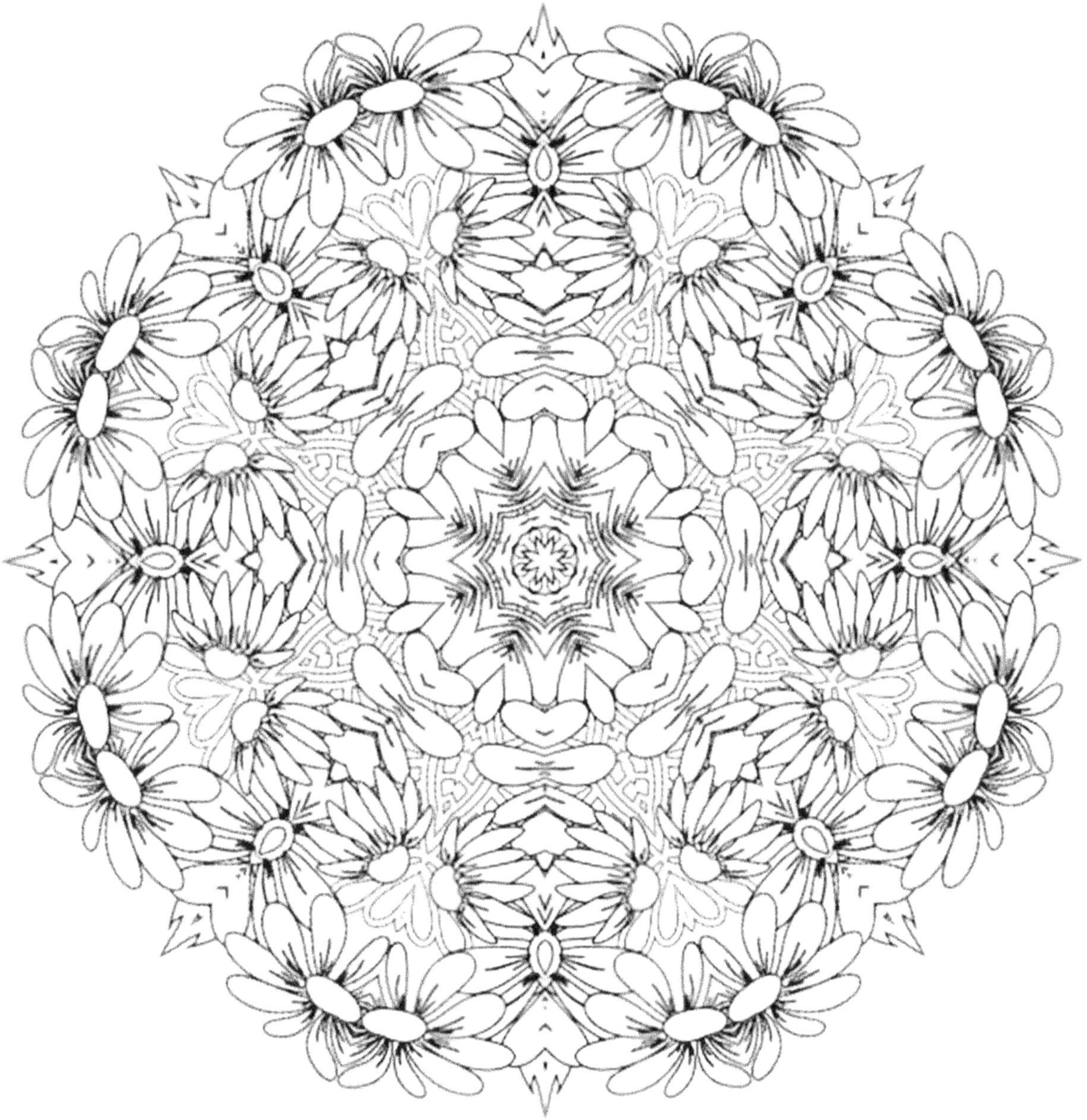

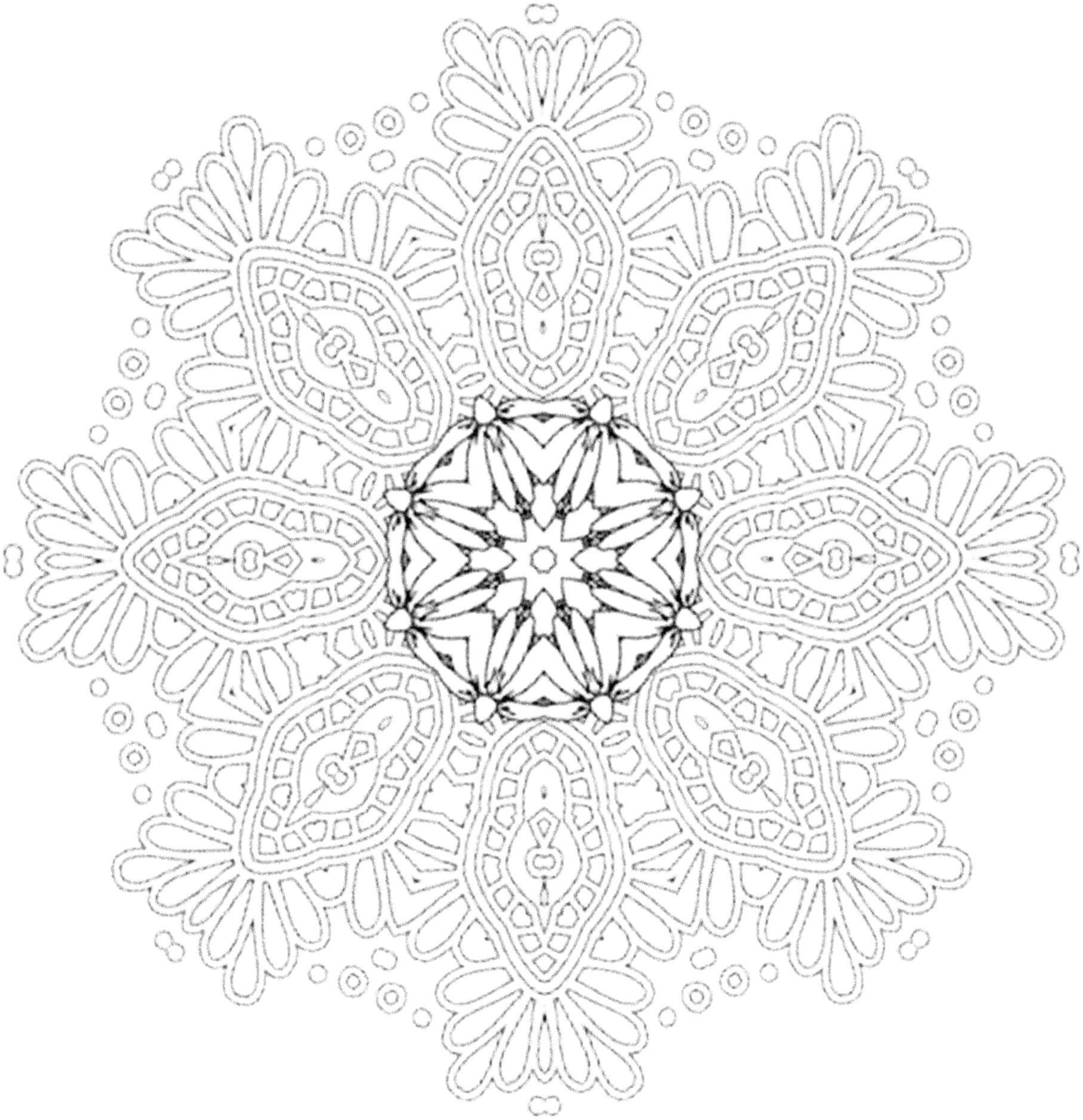

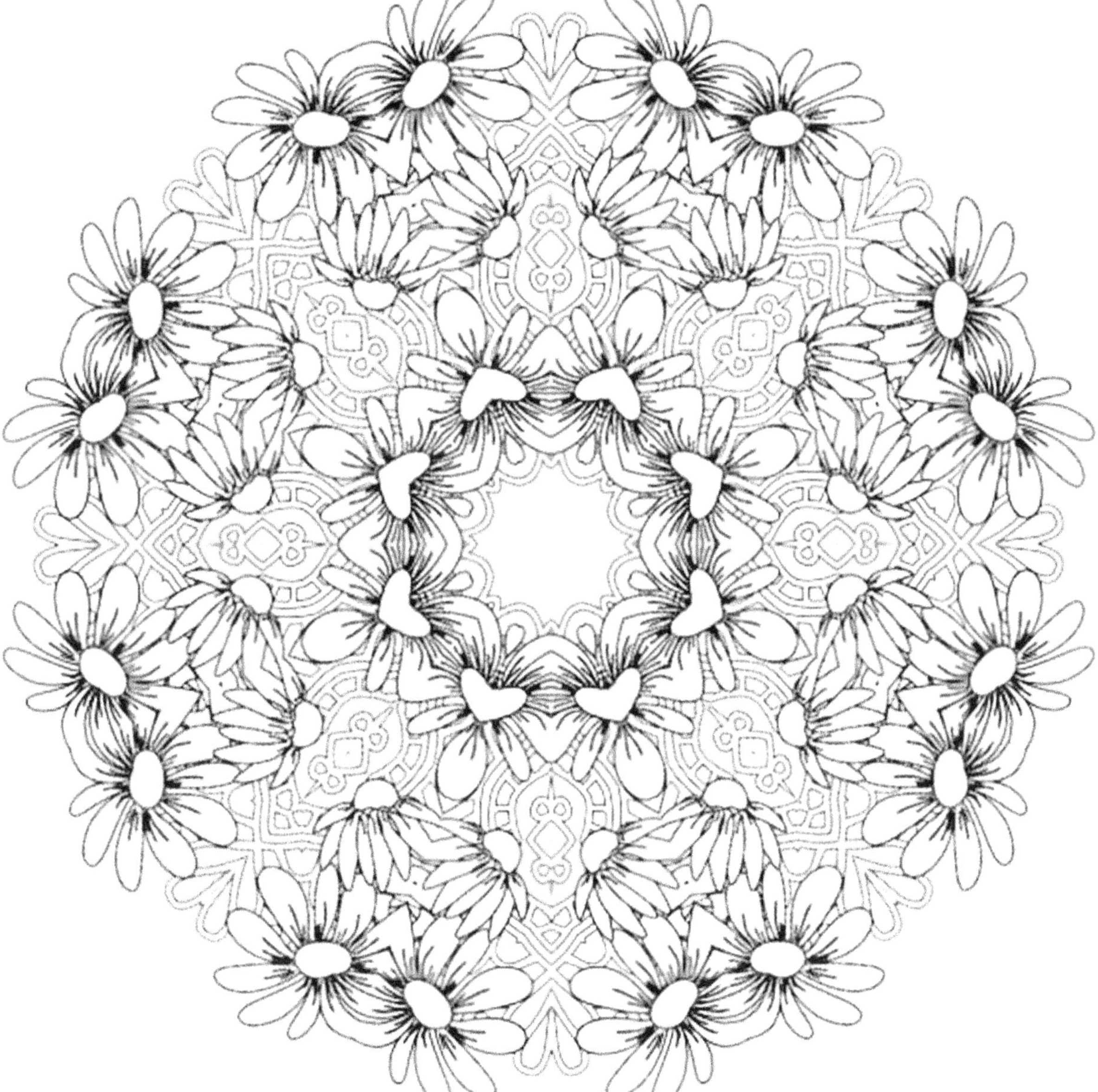

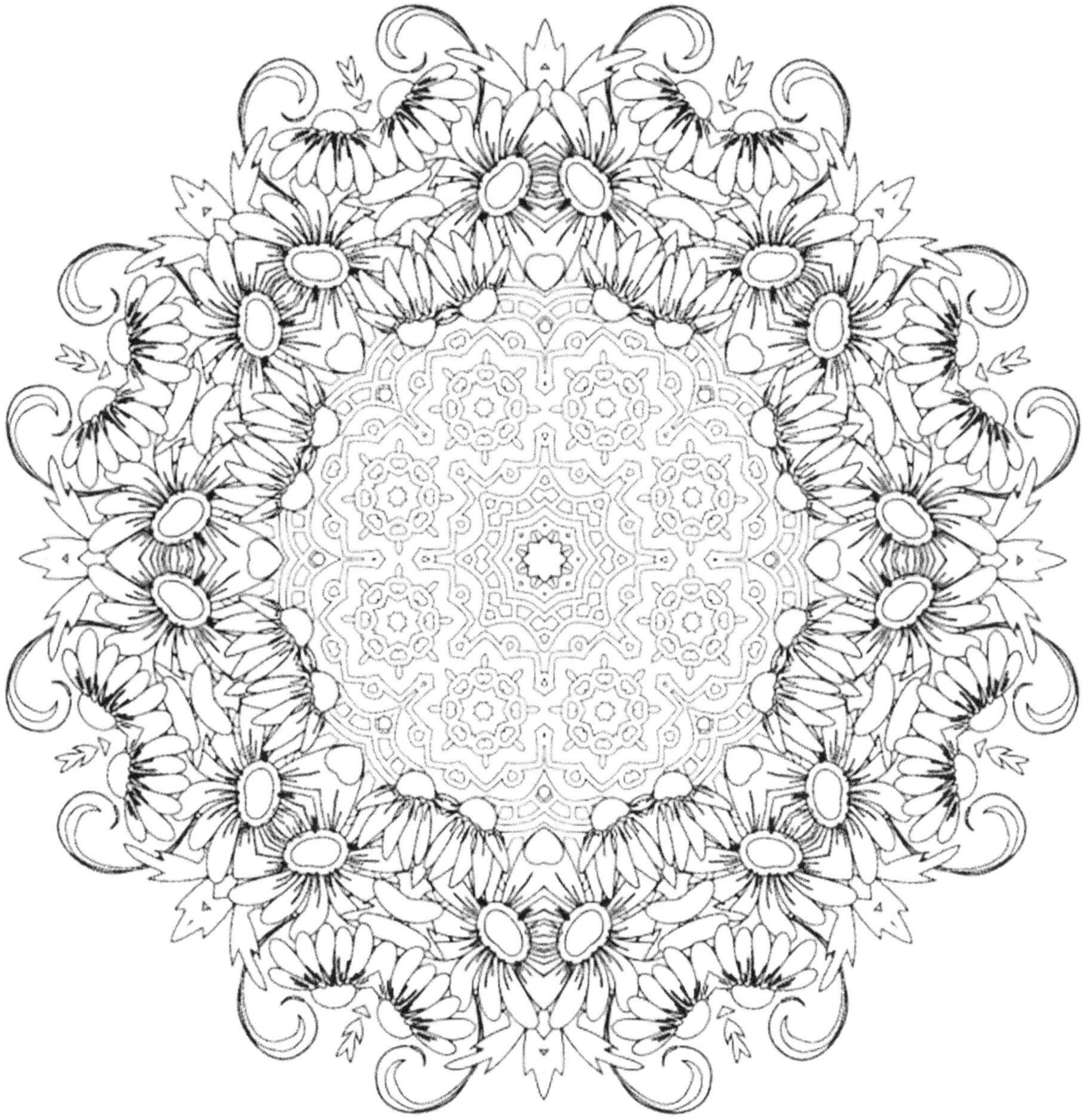

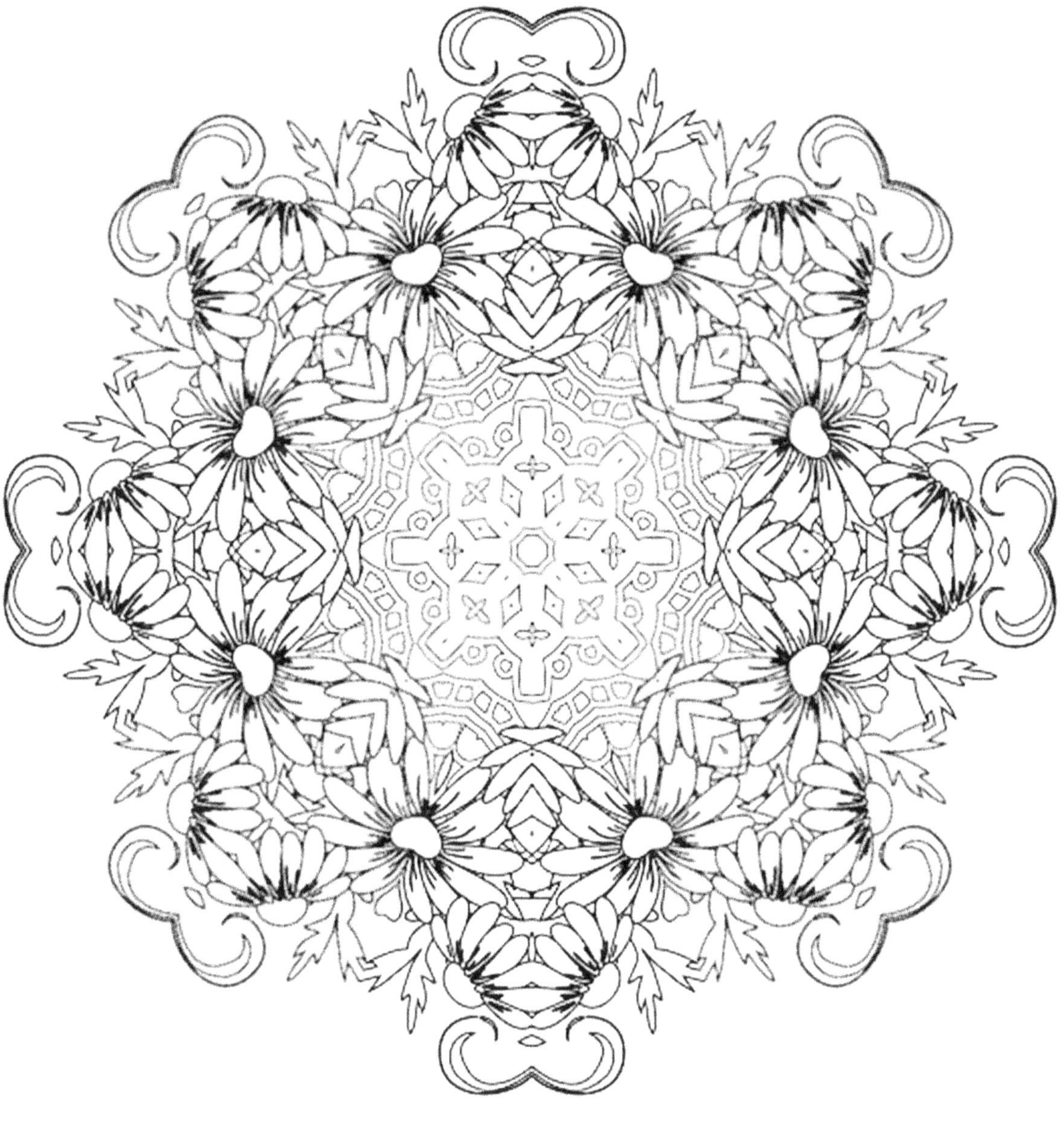

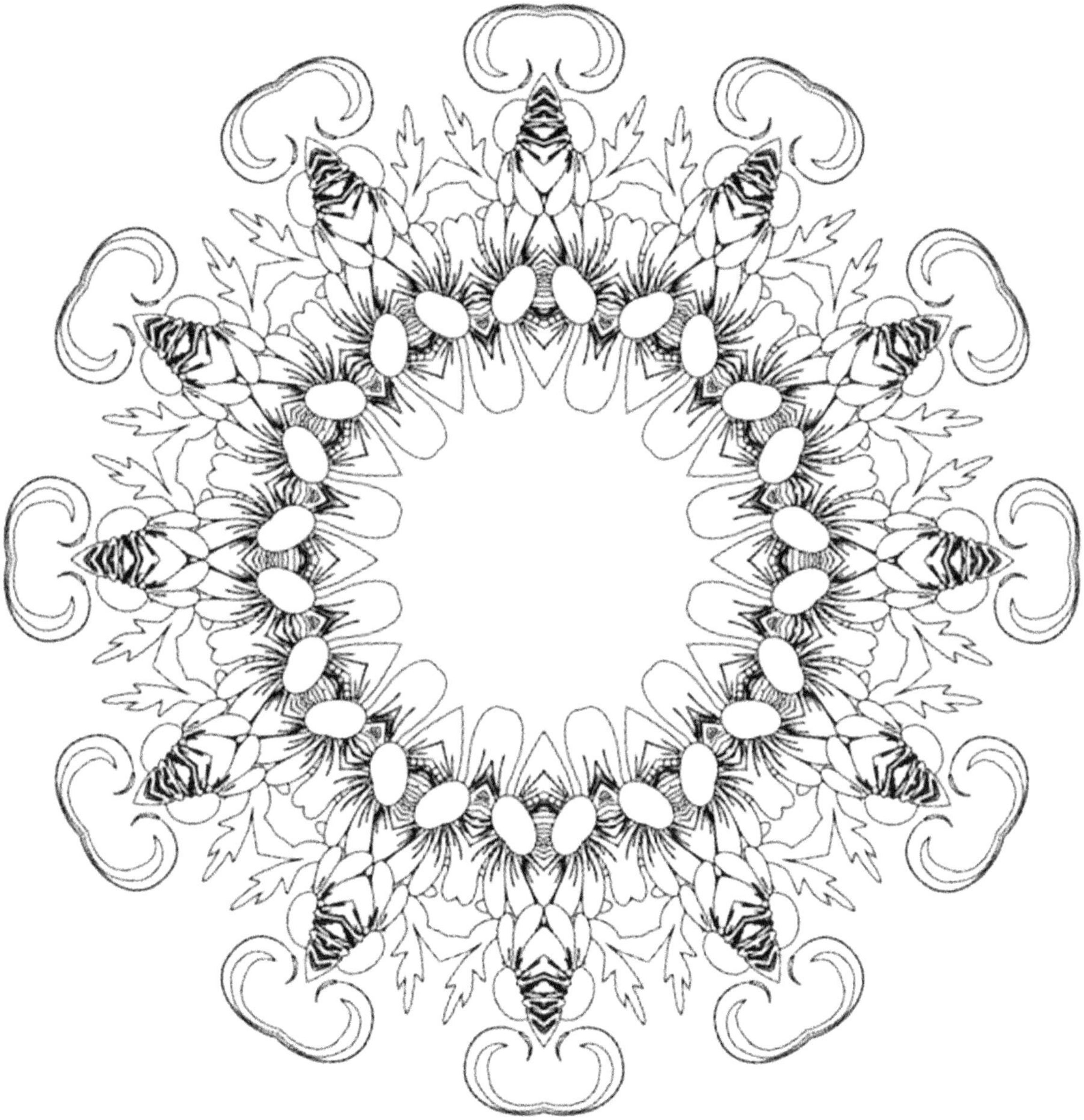

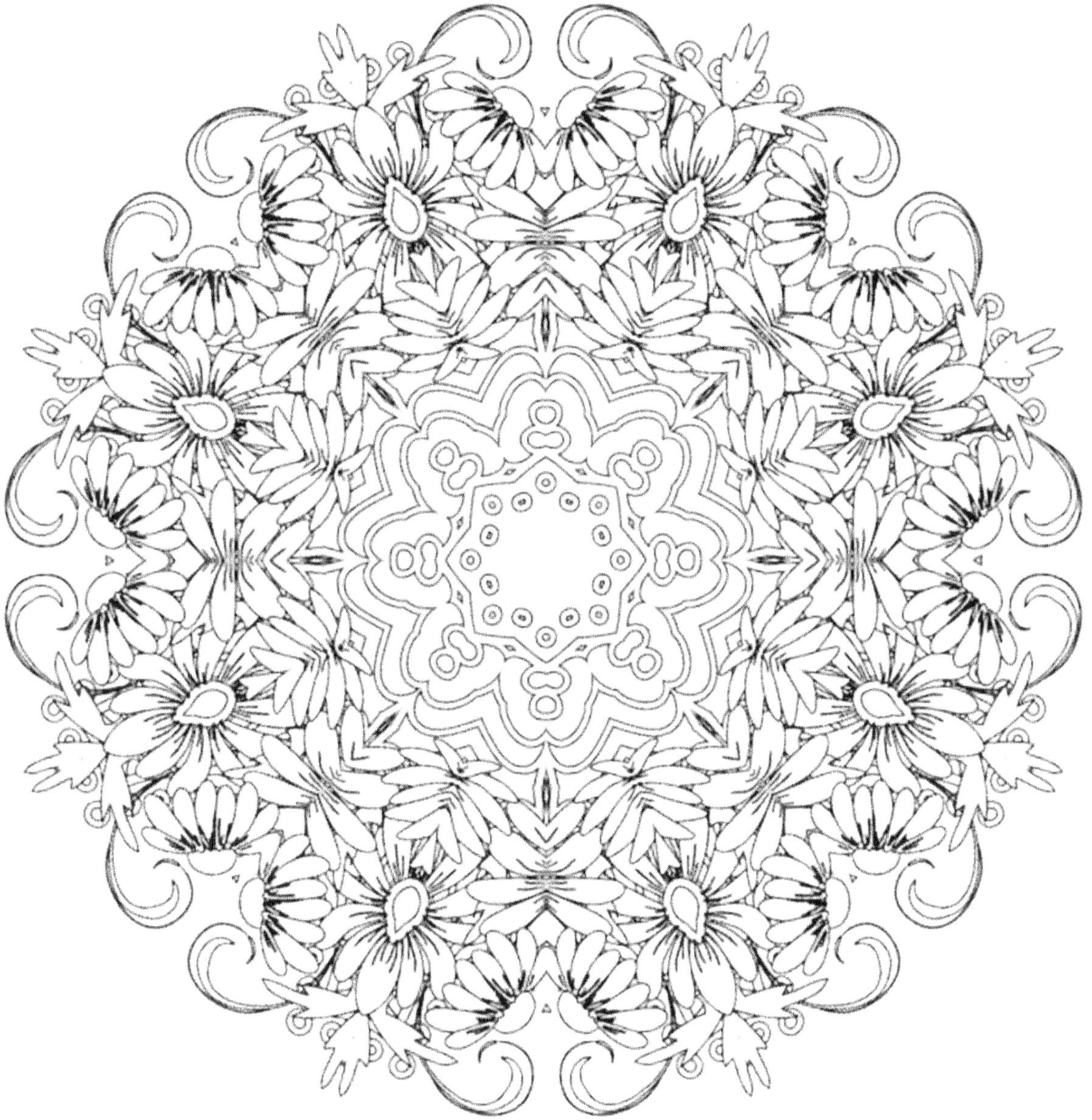

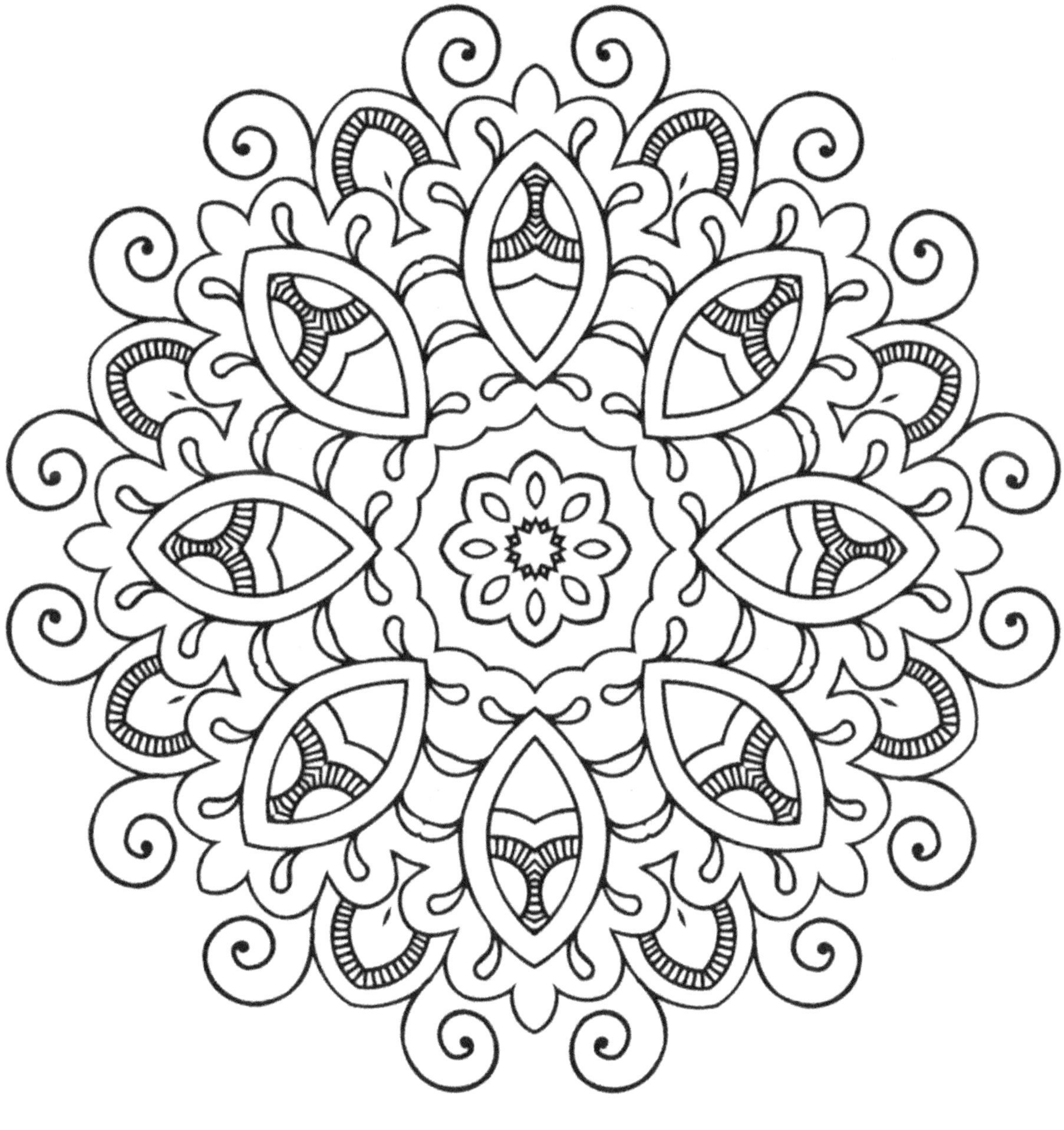

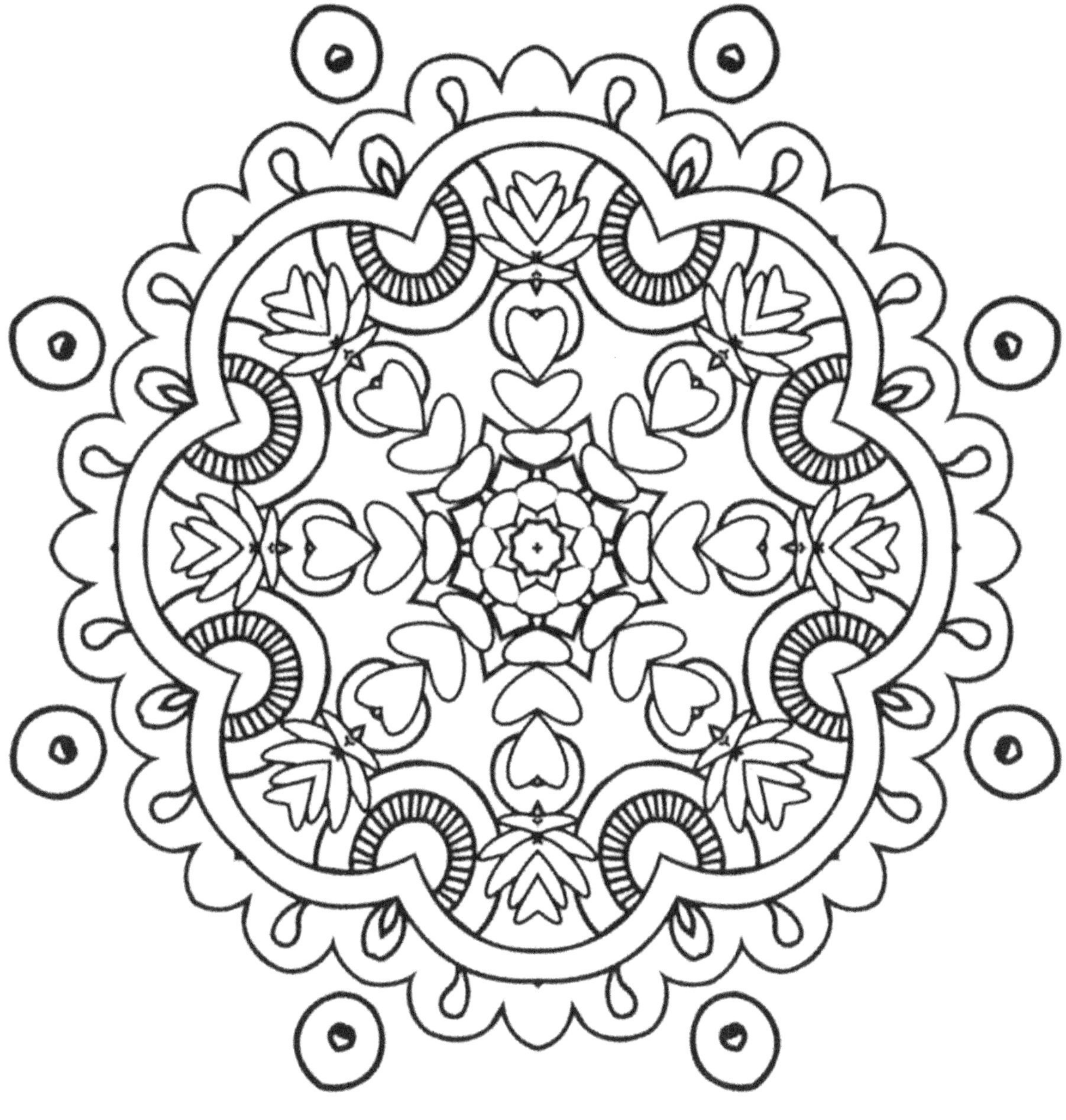

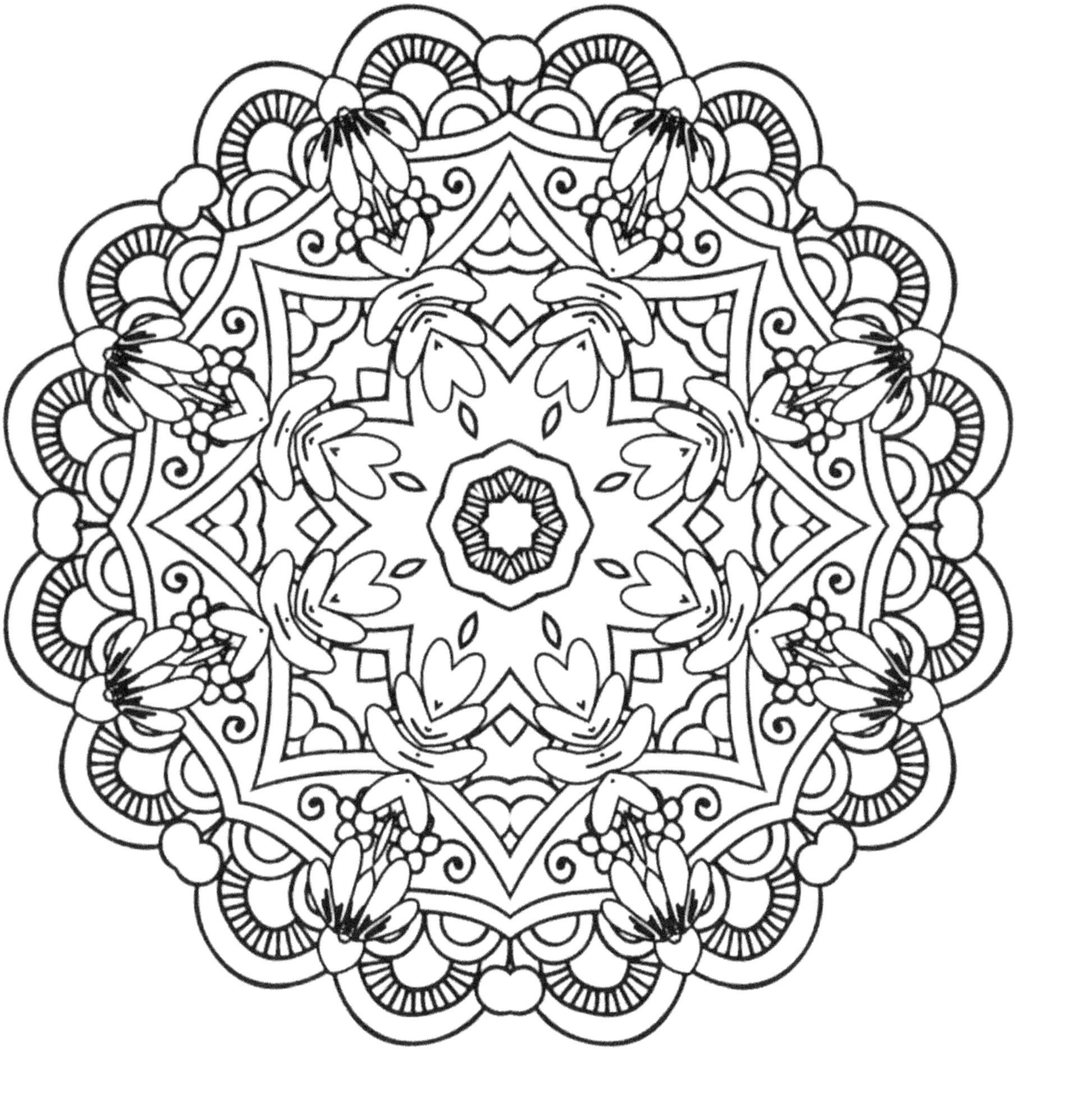

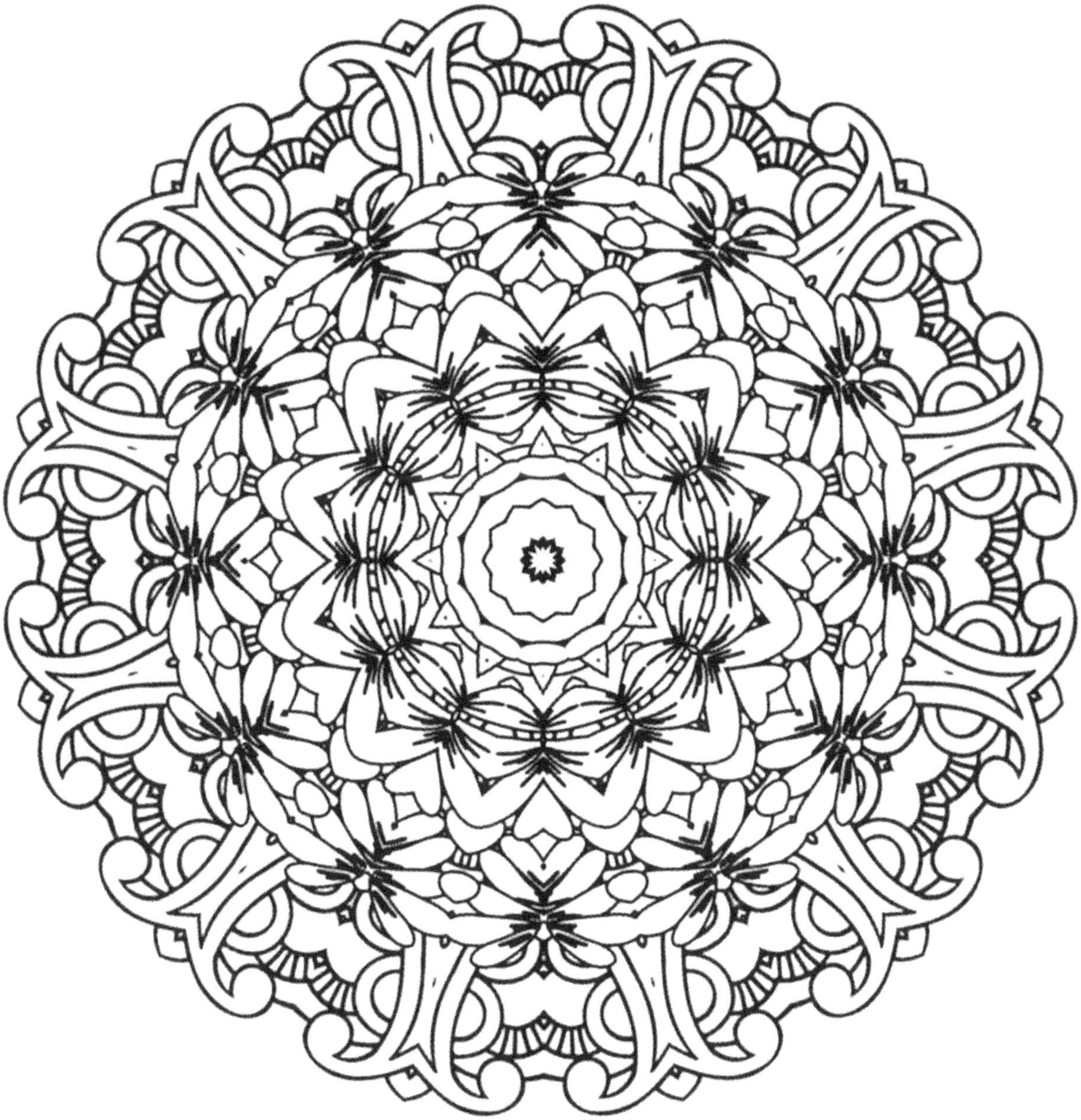

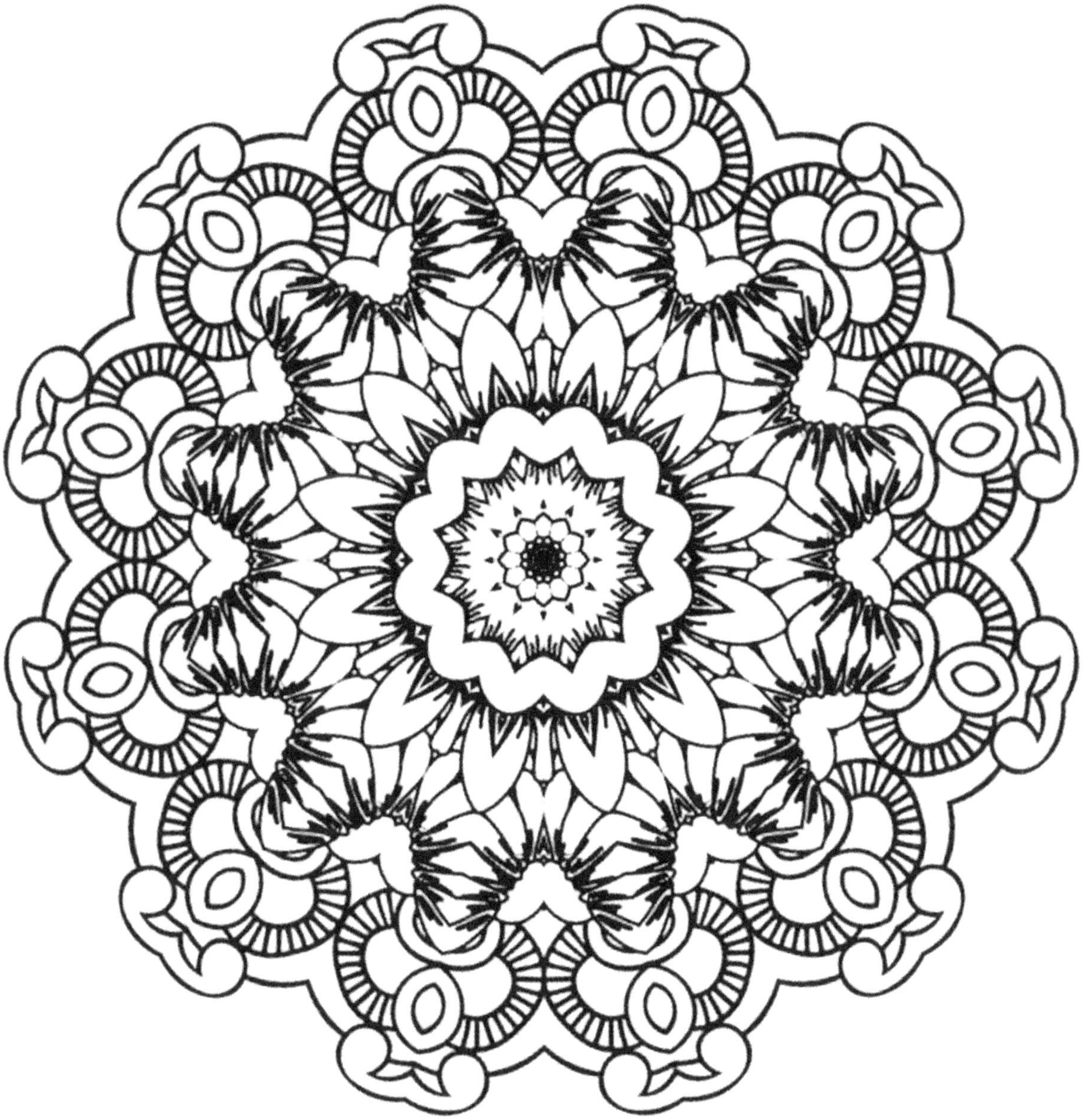

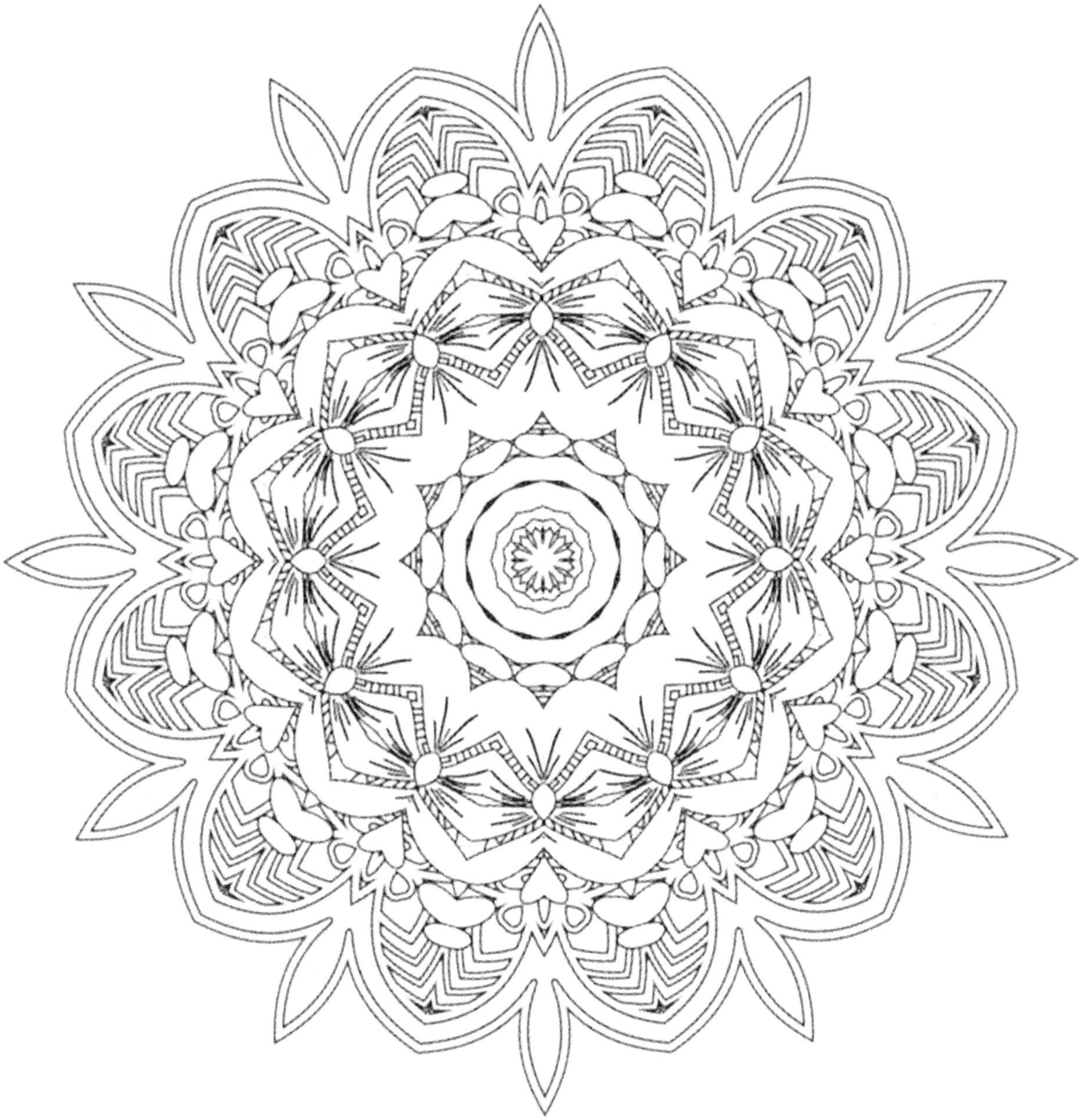

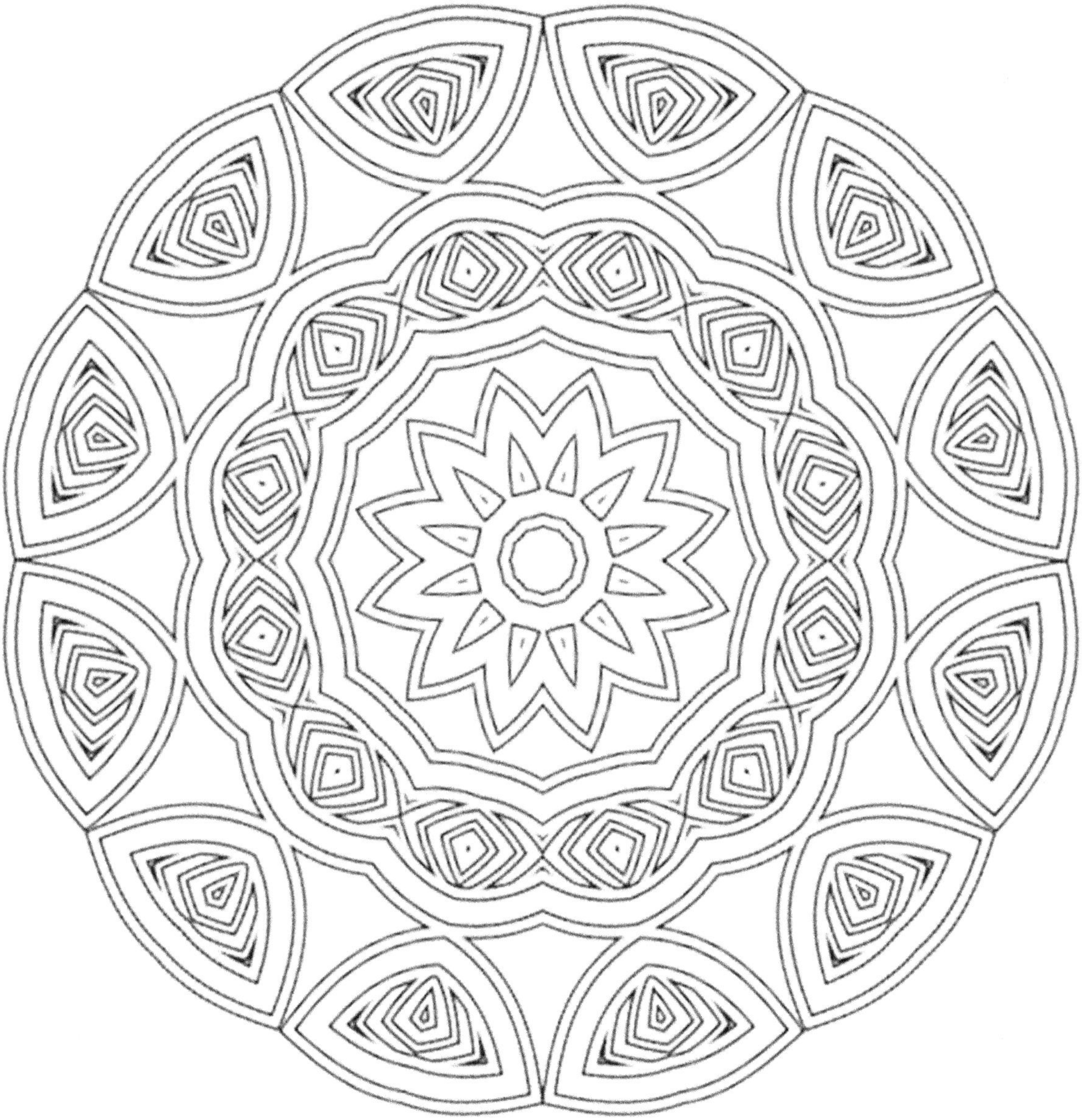

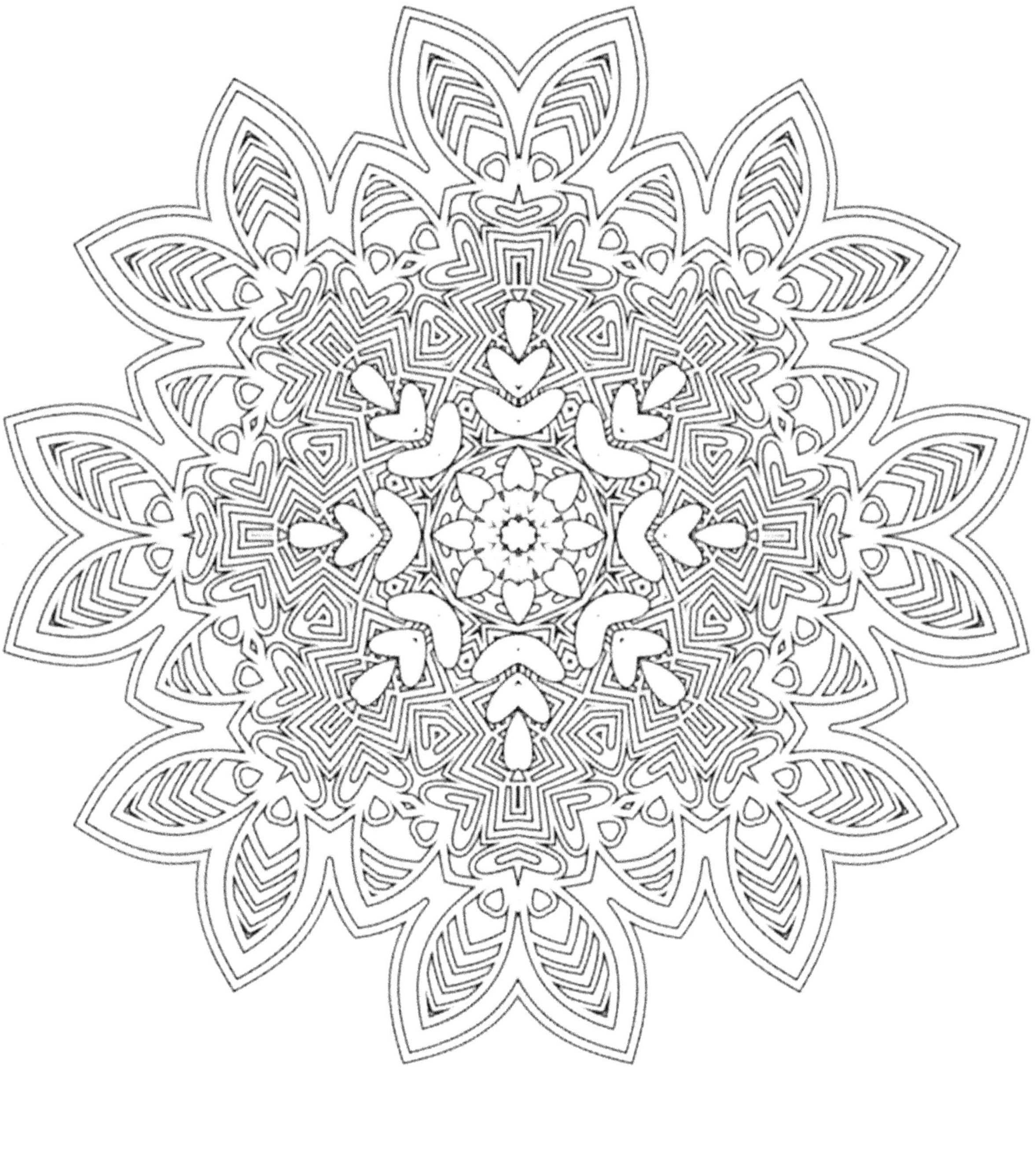

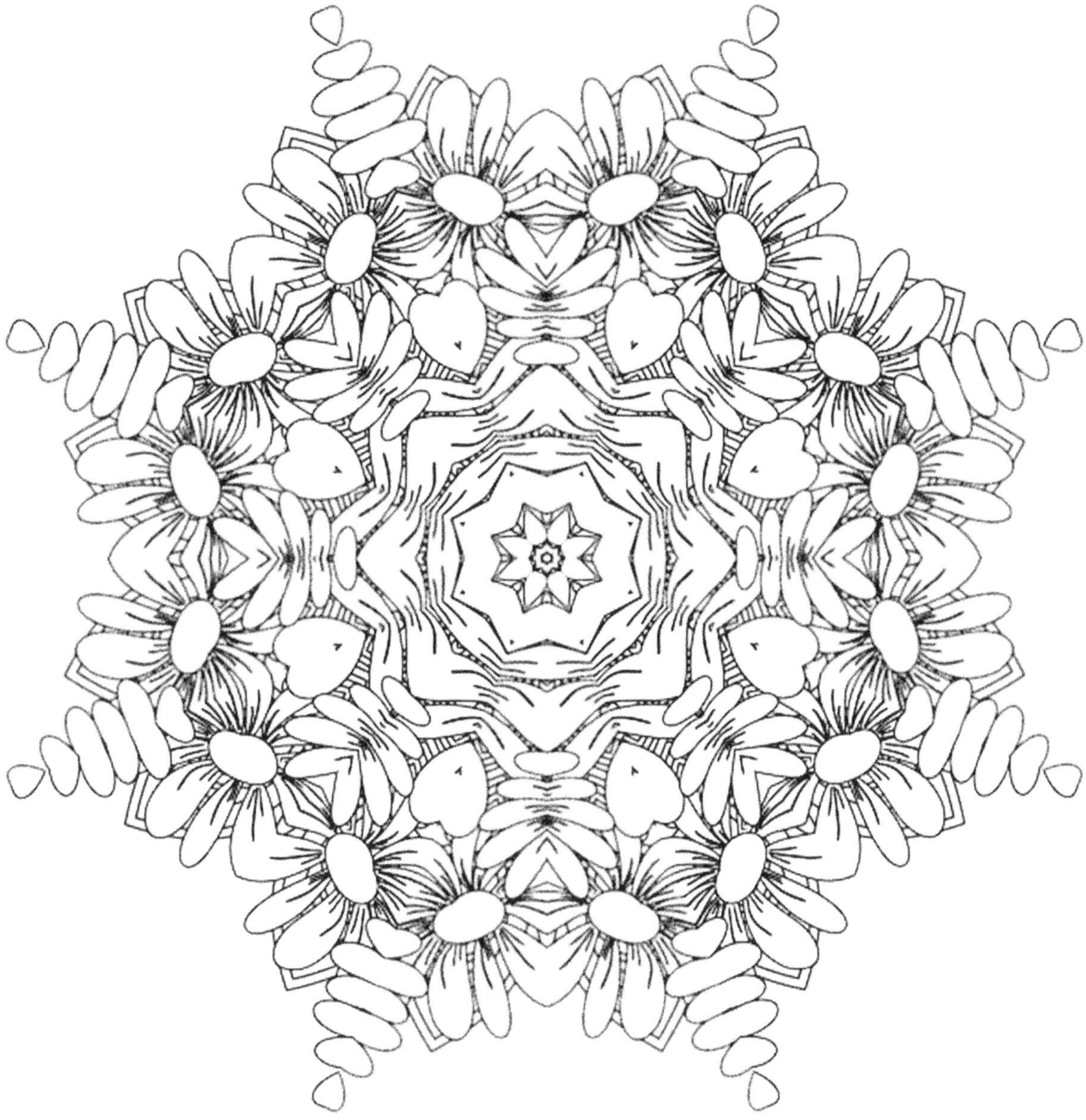

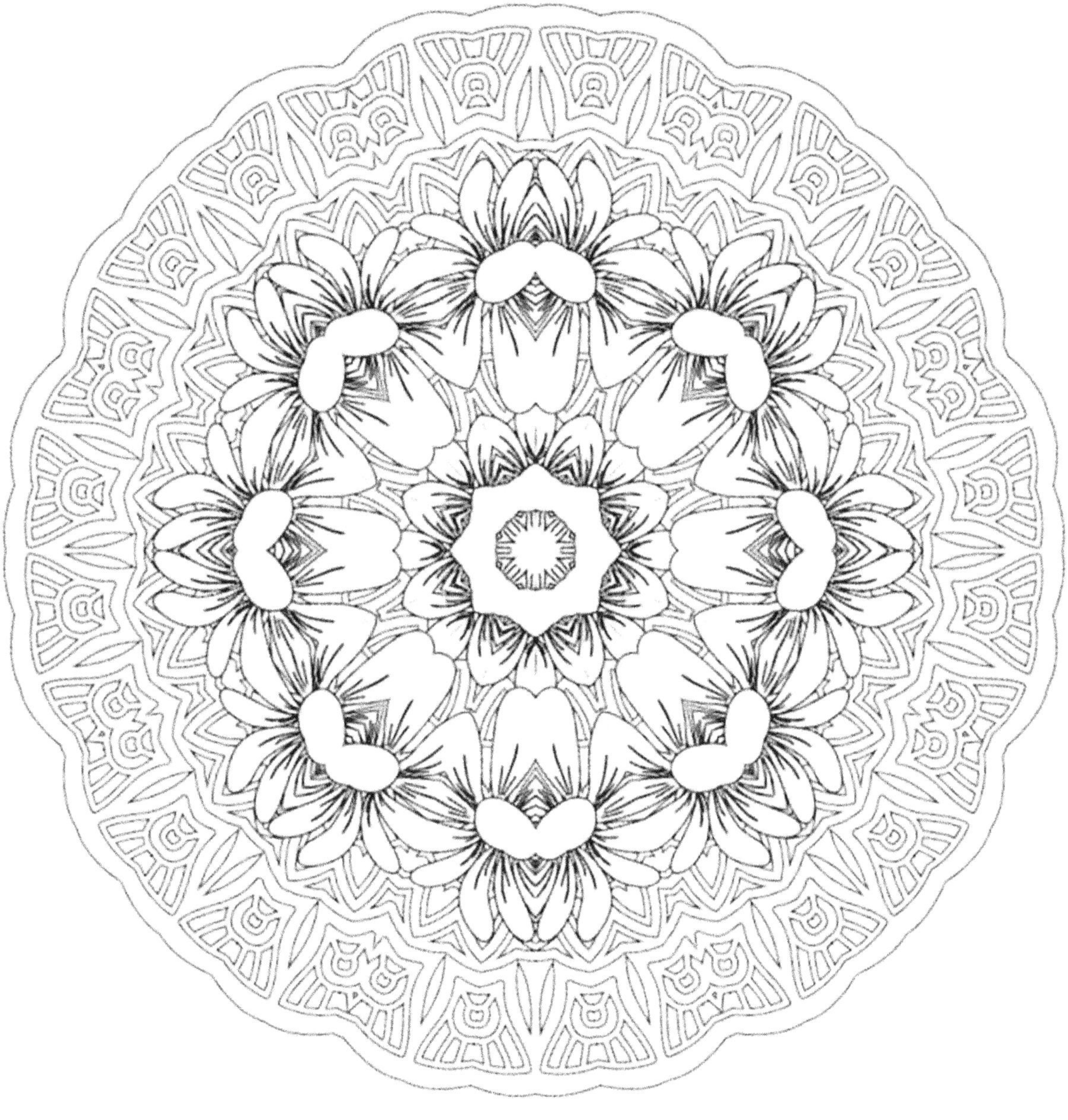

www.ingramcontent.com/pod-product-compliance
Lightning Source LLC
Chambersburg PA
CBHW080544190526
45169CB00007B/2635
9781537180540